How to Make Smart Decisions About Training

Save Money, Time, & Frustration

How to Make Smart Decisions About Training

Save Money, Time, & Frustration

Paul G. Whitmore, Ph.D.

CEP Press
A wholly owned subsidiary of
The Center for Effective Performance, Inc.
Atlanta, Georgia

OTHER BOOKS PUBLISHED BY CEP PRESS

Making an Impact: Building a Top-Performing Organization from the Bottom Up, by Timm J. Esque

Preparing Instructional Objectives, Third Edition, by Robert F. Mager

Analyzing Performance Problems, Third Edition, by Robert F. Mager & Peter Pipe

Making Instruction Work, Second Edition, by Robert F. Mager

What Every Manager Should Know About Training, by Robert F. Mager

For more information, contact:
CEP Press
2300 Peachford Rd.
Suite 2000
Atlanta, GA 30338
www.ceppress.com
(770) 458-4080 or (800) 558-4CEP

ISBN 1-879618-20-6

Library of Congress Catalog Card Number: 00-131785

Printed in the United States of America
09 08 07 06 05 04 03 02 01 10 9 8 7 6 5 4 3 2 1

Dedication

This book is dedicated to the trainers and training managers who are usually surrounded by people who are unaware of the craft of training as a potent technology. The tools in this book can help training personnel inform those they work with of the full potential of quality corporate training. Use these tools to transform your world into one where your craft is understood and valued.

Contents

Acknowledgments

The way this book came to be written reveals a great deal about how to write a book. And that's a secret I would like to share with my readers.

It all began when I was preparing for one of the Mager Associates/Center for Effective Performance "almost annual" Update Conferences. Bob Mager asked me to repeat some presentations I had made in previous years on training scams. I decided that instead of re-exposing training scams, I would present an algorithm for avoiding them.

That's what I did. And when I was finished, friends took over.

Seth Leibler said, "I want that."

Bob Mager advised, "Don't let anyone have it until you have written a book manuscript around it."

So I wrote a manuscript and sent it to my friends for review.

Bob Mager did yeoman cut-and-paste service, forcing me to cut or relocate some of my favorite topics that had little to do with the principal focus of the manuscript.

Ann Parkman helped me identify the technical foggy bottoms and blow the fog away, and gave me the idea of developing a tool kit based on the algorithm. That effort is still going on.

Paula Alsher suggested the principal tool—the worksheet. And she also sprinkled some exciting chapter titles here and there in the manuscript. Valerie Gernazian sharpened my dull points, and Don Richards brought impact to the work in many ways. Jill Russell edited the final version, digging confusions out of crevices and polishing overall. And, finally, "The Committee" (Ann Parkman, Suzanne Bennett, Vicki Chin, and Mark Steudel) ensured that all was realistic and practical and made sense.

Here is the secret I learned.
If you want to write a book:

1. Get an idea.

2. Gather some bright and talented friends and tell them your idea.

3. Take notes and do what your friends tell you to do.

4. Show them your draft and ask for their insights.

5. Make the changes they suggest.

6. Repeat steps 4 and 5 until your manuscript is ready for publication.

Perhaps the author line should read: "Paul Whitmore and friends."

Introduction

In the past, technology has been the competitive edge in business. Success has often been determined by how companies use technology to develop and produce products and services. In today's global marketplace, however, nearly all corporations are technology-oriented. So what differentiates the highly successful corporations from the "also-rans" in today's business world? Human performance.

Human performance is the new competitive edge, yet relatively few upper-level managers and executives realize that there is also a technology for developing and managing human performance. The question then becomes: how can we increase the power, productivity, and initiative of the employees in our companies? The quick answer is training. The correct answer is *the right kind of training.* The right kind of training is a powerful force and can turn a failed program into one that promotes tangible change.

Once training was a routine activity for corporations, a ho-hum matter often considered unimportant or useless—certainly not a priority. Today training is the most powerful tool upper management can use to achieve its most critical corporate strategies. Training is a multibillion-dollar industry staffed by highly talented professionals. Good training today can be much more effective than many executives have ever experienced.

A Decision Toolkit

Two factors have led to the increased significance of training to corporations around the world:

1. Changes in the nature and significance of work in corporations.

2. Incredible improvements in the effectiveness of training processes.

Most executives are aware of the first factor, but few know as much about the second one. In fact, most executives and upper-level managers have outdated beliefs about what training looks like and how well it can work.

Upper-level managers and executives need to learn how to tap the resources of the newly emerging human performance technologists, just as they learned in past years how to use the expertise of financial specialists, systems designers and engineers, production engineers, network engineers, and marketing specialists. Upper-level managers and executives do not need to become performance technologists themselves, but they do need to know when to call human performance technologists in on a problem, what to expect of them, and what kind of support to provide them.

The people who design and deliver the training have also changed. Not so long ago, trainers were employees drafted from line jobs. Those kinds of trainers are still around, but more and more trainers are professionals committed to a career in the training field. All of these changes have created a demand for highly effective and efficient training far beyond the capabilities of our traditional subject matter and performance augmented approaches typically found in our academic and vocational schools. Unfortunately, even today's professional trainers have not themselves been trained in the most effective and efficient training development technology. Most of the professional training schools are still a generation behind the technology available in the market today.

Changes in the Nature and Significance of Work

First, new technologies have greatly improved the quality and quantity of goods and services produced by individual workers. The impact of one worker today, for good or for bad, far exceeds the impact of a half dozen or more workers in past decades. Consequently, every worker must be fully competent for the company to be competitive.

Second, many day-to-day management decisions have been moved from managers to the employees who provide the service or product. This means faster responses to rapidly changing technology and global market conditions. It also eliminates some levels of management. It makes a corporation much more competitive given today's customer expectations. If a corporation today doesn't meet customers' quality and service expectations, another corporation will, and the first will lose significant market share—perhaps enough to put it out of business.

These kinds of changes require that employees be equipped with new skills and new ways of thinking about their jobs. This means training, very effective training that prepares employees for the new strategies very quickly. Many corporations have failed to implement change strategies successfully because they relied on antiquated training approaches.

There is also an increasing demand for high skill jobs—so called "knowledge" jobs. This is the new capital of today—human capital. Rarely does human capital come fully developed. Instead, corporations have to develop their employees through training, performance, and mentoring programs.

Improved productivity, new management structures and practices, and new business strategies all focus on human performance. Human performance is critical to their effective implementation. Employees have to change how they do their jobs and even how they think about them. That means new job skills, new job incentives, and new ways of interacting with each other.

Effectiveness in Training

What change has occurred in training to meet this greatly increased demand for training effectiveness? The computer? Biochemical nutrients for workers? Nothing so trite. A different kind of training: criterion-referenced instruction (CRI). CRI was developed out of behavioral science research by Dr. Robert F. Mager and Peter Pipe (1994), leading figures in the performance improvement industry. CRI meets the challenge by reengineering the instructional process to fit the needs and circumstances of today's businesses and industries. The magic comes from different ways of thinking about the purposes and processes of instruction—ways that have long been employed in other business activities. What are they?

- Clearly defining and measuring the desired outcomes of a process (the criteria) as a basis for designing and operating the process.

- Applying modern production concepts and practices to the development of skills in individual employees. (The job isn't done until it is done right, or the learning isn't over until the student performs to job criteria.)

- Focusing on what students do rather than on what instructors do. First, we decide on what changes need to be made to the product (the student), and then we decide on what the production line (instructional process) and worker (the instructor) need to do to make that happen.

Changing how we think is far more difficult than simply adopting new ways of doing old things. We are not simply learning to use a new tool. Instead, we are focusing on new goals that we were not able to realize in the past and using old tools, as well as new ones, to accomplish what we could not accomplish before.

Is it scientific? Its roots are in behavioral science. But new rationales for it are emerging from the latest of our sciences—neuroscience, the science of how the brain works. CRI is in complete accord with this very latest science.

Training and human resources personnel are usually the ones to educate the corporation of the existence and power of performance technology. This book is written principally for training managers and HR directors to enhance their knowledge of CRI.

"How Do I Know Which Training Is Best?"

The heart of this book is *The Path to Smart Training Decisions* flowchart and worksheet, which leads you through the process of evaluating proposed training programs. Think of it as your map to the greatest value in training. It will lead you to the training "gold" every time.

The Path to Smart Training Decisions flowchart and worksheet is particularly useful when deciding between two or more proposals for meeting the same training requirement. While training proposals can differ in several ways, the flowchart and worksheet helps you arrive at a single value for each proposal. This makes it easy to show each proposal's value relative to the others and, more importantly, allows you to document and defend your selection to other levels of management.

Chapter 1 provides an overview of the rationales and major processes of CRI. Chapters 2–10 each focus on one of the nine steps of *The Path to Smart Training Decisions*, explaining the concept behind each step and giving guidance on what to look for and avoid. Chapters 11 and 12 give tips on how to use *The Path to Smart Training Decisions* worksheet and advice on how to present the concept of CRI and garner support from various corporate audiences. Training and HR personnel do not operate alone in a corporation. They have to be able to gather support from those around them and from those in higher levels of management. Consequently, in the appendices, there are several tools that can help in gaining support from upper management or non-training managers. These articles and charts can help to stimulate and guide discussion of issues that are often significant in obtaining others' support. They include the following:

- A comparison of two *Instructional Paradigms*: the business paradigm and the academic paradigm. The academic paradigm is most common in our society. Most people do not know that there is another paradigm designed specifically to meet business needs. This comparison may be especially useful in helping you gain support from non-training managers and upper management. It can also help with trainees accustomed to, and wary of, the academic paradigm.

- A comparison of the old and new views of *How People Really Learn (With Implications for Training)*. The new view is based on the latest findings from neuroscience on how the brain works. These findings and their implications are neither well-known nor well-understood by most of the public, including professional trainers. This comparison may be especially useful in helping you gain support from non-training managers and upper management.

- A short article, "Criterion-Referenced Instruction for Today's Business Needs," describes the general characteristics of CRI. This benefits-oriented piece is written for non-training personnel, especially upper-level executives, who need to quickly get up to speed on this topic.

The Path to Smart Training Decisions will help you *recognize*—both during the development process and after it is finished—training that works. It will lead you through the development of a training program: outlining the questions you need to ask along the way and the answers to expect.

Chapter 1

What You Need to Know Before You Buy

Does a training program have to be developed and evaluated before you know whether it will work? Are there practices you can look at before or during the development of the program that will predict its success or failure? Must buying training be the same as buying a "pig in a poke," or can you peek before you pay? The answer is that, not only can you peek, you can take a long, hard look and discover everything you need to know— if you know what to look for.

Why is it important to know what to look for in training before you buy? Because the field of training is filled with vendors and practitioners who think they know how people learn and perform, but don't. The problem is compounded by the fact that many managers and executives are also ignorant of how people learn and perform, often because they have accepted the popular views of unknowing vendors and consultants. Are these people running training scams? Usually not. The end result, however, is the same: the customer pays good money for training that does not work. The customer not only loses money and time, but also risks jeopardizing important business strategies that rely on a trained workforce to implement.

Typically, a program will be administered and then evaluated to determine whether it is worth continuing and whether the source is a trustworthy source for effective training programs in the future. But evaluation at this point is often too late. Many of these programs are just one piece in a critical change project in the corporation. Failure of the training program undermines the larger project. The corporation is left scrambling to fix it or forget it. All too often, the corporation chooses the latter and limps on.

Why are there so many training programs that don't work? The best known science in the training field, on which most training methodologies have been built, is based on the idea that the brain works like a computer. However, in recent years, neuroscience has established that the brain as computer metaphor is false, and a second generation of cognitive science, based on how the brain really works, is taking hold. This has enormous implications for training; if methodologies have been built from incorrect assumptions about how the brain works, our technologies for teaching people are not going to be as effective as they need to be.

Mager and Pipe's criterion-referenced instruction, the methodology on which *The Path to Smart Training Decisions* is based, is the only training methodology that is fully consistent with the latest findings on how the brain actually works. However, this second generation science constitutes a major paradigm shift. Consequently, it is still being resisted, which is why professional schools in training do not include the latest, most effective, and least complicated training development methodology. It is not surprising that the most effective, practical, and least complicated technology turns out to be the most scientifically valid.

Brain Fallacies and Brain Truths: How They Affect Training

Training programs are intended to produce desired learning, and learning happens inside the brain. Our culture is fraught with misconceptions and myths regarding the workings of the mind. It's important that you, the customer, know the truth to protect yourself from well-meaning but ignorant purveyors of training programs and philosophies. This section briefly describes the major findings from the relatively young field of neuroscience on how learning happens.

Academic instruction has always been based on ignorance and suppositions about the nature of the raw material with which it works—the human brain. Until about twenty years ago, relatively little was known about how our brains worked. Behavioral scientists put the brain in a black box in the mid-1920s, and it has remained there until just recently. Thirty years ago, cognitive scientists sought to make the brain a legitimate object for research. One of their key assumptions was that the brain functioned like a computer. They then proceeded to build unnecessarily complex theories of mind and memory based on this assumption, which turned out to be erroneous.

In recent years, some of those same cognitive scientists have joined biologists, neurologists, and philosophers to finally open the black box. They found that the brain is like an elegant and intricate switching system, building neural circuits that connect sensory inputs to motor and glandular outputs. Performances are shaped by pathways of neurons in our brains. Clusters of neurons called neural networks perform specific functions by receiving incoming signals and routing those signals to other clusters. If you think of each cluster of neurons as a pearl, then the pathways are like strings of pearls tied together into great nets. The networks have so many layers that the pathways through our brains are like superhighways with thousands of intertwining lanes. Pathways can also be changed in much the same way that railroad track feeders can be switched from one continuing track to another. Like the connect-the-dot puzzles we did as children, our brains connect neurons or clusters of neurons to generate the performances we need to learn to do.

Neuroscience has clearly established that our brains do not work like the computers we build (Edelman 1992). We cannot move information around as you could do in a computer. Our brains do not contain extensive memories in which we can store massive amounts of knowledge and retrieve items whenever we need them. Nor is there a record in our brains of all the things that have ever happened to us. Our traditional concepts of memory are flat-out wrong.

We remember largely by talking to ourselves about an event while it is happening and afterwards. Our perceptions stimulate the words, and the words in turn elicit mental imagery. We rehearse these verbal and visual *performances*, and they become our *record* of the event. Bits and pieces of these records are used in many other performances and are changed in the process. When next we "remember," we use those bits and pieces that have changed in small ways. That's partly how we misremember (Loftus 1997).

Hebb's Law is one of the cornerstones of neuroscience. It is often stated in this way: "Neurons that fire together wire together." In practical terms, this means that we learn when we do the same behavior in the same way repeatedly. The connections among neurons are strengthened whenever they fire together. All you need to do to get your employees to learn how to do their jobs is to get them to practice doing the skills they need on their jobs. Such practice ensures that the right neurons fire together.

To guide your employees through learning these skills, you must:

- Specify what it is you want them to learn to do.

- Develop situations that lead them through *doing* the things you want them to learn to do.

- Create learning experiences that lead your employees to have consistently positive feelings (but not high excitement) associated with the things they are learning to do. Pay attention to your employees' feelings during training. Improper feelings experienced during learning can lead employees to make improper decisions later on the job. High anxiety and high excitement disrupt effective learning and working.

What Should Effective Training Look Like?

Suppose you are manufacturing a product in which each item is made by a single crafts worker. Your product requires a lot of rework in the field after it is delivered to the customer. Field reps have to go in and fix this part, replace that one, and adjust another. Some items never work well, depending on which crafts worker made them. Such inefficiency is costing you all of your profits. Your initial approach to dealing with this problem is to find ways to do the rework more efficiently—do it faster at lower cost. That's the academic approach.

A far more efficient approach is to deal with the problem at its source: the manufacturing process. You assign crafts workers to those jobs they do best. You invest in the development of a largely automated assembly line. Every single item you ship falls within specified quality standards. Rework in the field is down to zero, and you are keeping all of your profits.

Traditional training methods resemble the academic experiences we were exposed to in school: information is presented in textbooks and lectures, and each student decides what to study and how. Students are tested on what they learned and assigned grades based on their test performance. The students seldom are able to recall what they learned and apply it on the job. Even the "A" students go through a long learning period on the job (the infamous "learning curve") after the program has ended.

Training programs that follow the criterion-referenced model (CRI) provide a much different experience, with much better results. The focus of the training is on performance[1] rather than subject matter. Employees *practice* performing the mental and physical skills required on the job, instead of being presented with information in textbooks and lectures. There are no grades or tests in the conventional sense. A "test" consists of the instructor observing an employee to see if he or she has achieved competence in a skill. Each employee practices each skill until he or she achieves competence. When job competence is verified, the employee moves on to the next skill. Every employee who meets the program's performance criteria or standards succeeds in the program *and* on the job. Because employees must demonstrate competence in the skill as part of training, every employee is fully competent on the job at completion of the training program, rather than two or three months later (or more), as is often the case with traditional training programs.

If you look in on a CRI-based program, you will rarely see employees sitting in rows of chairs facing the front of the room watching and listening to a glitzy media presentation or expert lecturer. Instead, there may be several small clusters of employees helping each other practice, or employees working alone. One or two may be watching a short video demonstrating a skill. Different employees might be practicing many different skills, depending on where they are in the program and what they need to learn or practice at the moment. Several instructors may be moving about in the area, reviewing individual employees' practice, and coaching them on how to improve performance. The instructors are skilled performers and expert coaches. When lectures are used to prepare students to practice, they are short and focus on a few specific skills. Employees practice the target skills immediately following each mini-lecture.

The training may not even take place in a classroom. It may happen on the production floor, in the employee's office, in the field, in a break room, or by computer. All the employees in a class might not even be at the same location at the same time. They may be scattered about at various places to support whatever activity they need to engage in at the time. There may not even be organized

---

1. The general term *performance instruction* is often used to specify training programs that contain substantial information (or knowledge) presentations, but in which the students are also required to apply that information to practical problems. Such programs are really performance-enhanced subject matter training. Such programs do *not* produce employees who are fully competent performers at the completion of the program. In *criterion-referenced instruction*, necessary information is presented immediately before practicing the skill in which the information will be applied, and only that information required by the skill is included in such presentations. Criterion-referenced instruction does indeed produce competent performers by the completion of the program.

classes of employees. They may enter the training program at times convenient to them and leave as they complete the training. Wherever and however it happens, the instruction (materials and instructors) will guide employees through practicing those skills they need to learn as effectively and efficiently as possible. The cost of the training will not exceed the value of the skills to the organization.

What drives this kind of training? Success, more than anything else. Success in each and every part of the training. Little successes and big successes. Employees are always prepared to learn whatever they are asked to learn. There is no failure. If an employee needs help or more practice, he or she gets it. Once an employee meets the standard on a skill, he or she moves on—and not before.

Criterion-referenced programs do not result in substantial learning curves on the job after graduation. Learning curves following traditional programs result from not teaching employees all the skills they need to succeed on the job or from not having employees practice such skills in realistic contexts. In CRI, because each employee practices each job skill in job-like conditions to job standards during training, training performance and job performance are the same. Complete transfer from the classroom to the job invariably follows, and graduates arrive at the job fully competent.

Good training today can be much better than the kind of instruction most of us experienced as we grew up. Most training being offered in and by corporations today, however, is still the traditional approach—a method that does not work well and leaves employees feeling anxious and fearful. How can you know in advance which one you are buying?

You will know by asking the right questions and recognizing the right answers about training. This book tells you how.

Using the Path to Smart Training Decisions

Savvy art buyers cannot always tell a masterpiece from a forgery just by looking at it, but they do know what questions to ask and who to call in when they need help. The same goes for savvy HR/training directors and managers. You cannot know everything, but you can protect yourself and your corporation by probing in the right areas and by knowing what you should and should not find.

The Path to Smart Training Decisions flowchart and worksheet ensures that the elements you need in your training program are there. You need to ask questions about training programs you are planning to have developed or programs you are considering purchasing to ensure that these phases will be or have been properly conducted.

You could be looking at one of several different types of programs:

■ Off-the-shelf programs provided by vendors;

■ Programs developed by the corporation's in-house trainers, training developers, line workers, supervisors, and managers; or

■ Programs developed under contract by external consultants.

Regardless of which type, *The Path to Smart Training Decisions* ensures the programs you provide to your company are fully criterion-referenced. That means they will produce graduates who are competent to perform the job for which they are trained when they graduate—not months or years later, but immediately. It ensures that the training programs are highly efficient— employees don't spend longer in the training program than is absolutely necessary to learn to do the job. And, finally, it ensures that trainees find the training process to be comfortable and free of anxiety and that they have confidence in the skills they learn.

The Path to Smart Training Decisions flowchart and worksheet appears in appendix D. In addition to appendix D, you will also find a foldout of the flowchart at the back of the book, so that you can reference it while going through the process. The flowchart and worksheet contains nine steps.

1. **Is There a Business Need?** Ensure that there is a significant business need to support the training.

2. **Is the Focus on Performance?** Ensure that there is a need for training—that is, there is something some employees are not *doing* (or are doing improperly) that they ought to be doing. And employees are failing to perform these functions *because they lack the necessary skills*. Ensure that the program is focused specifically on those skills the employees need.

3. **Are Tasks and Skills Detailed?** Ensure that specific job tasks and skills will be named and described in detail. Skills targeted for training are specified as measurable performances in real job conditions that meet a real job standard.

4. **Is Practice Realistic?** Ensure that employees will practice every needed skill in a realistic job format. There is an audit

trail that establishes how each skill and its characteristics were identified—including the sources of information and the procedures for obtaining the information.

5. **Does Practice Include a Mix of Job Situations?** Ensure that every employee will practice needed skills in a representative range of job situations.

6. **Do Learners Practice to Job Competence?** Ensure that every employee in the training program practices each and every skill as many times as he or she needs to practice it to achieve job competence of the skill.

7. **Does Practice Equal at Least Half of Training?** Ensure that the program is efficient. Employees spend at least half their time in the program practicing skills rather than preparing to practice. The program is free of extraneous content that does not support the practice of specific skills.

8. **Will Practices Cause Negative Feelings?** Ensure that the program is designed and administered to provide every employee who goes through it with a positive learning experience.

9. **Is the Program of Value?** Ensure that the program provides more benefit and value to the corporation than it costs to design, develop (or purchase), and deliver.

Each step in the flowchart consists of two to three blocks. The first block always contains the major question to be resolved in the step. If the major question is satisfied by the proposal, go directly to the next step in the flowchart. If the major question is not satisfied by the current proposal, the next block will usually ask if the shortcoming can be fixed. If the shortcoming cannot be fixed, go to the third block in the section, which tells you either to stop at this point or to proceed only if you have no other options.

Chapters 2–10 each address a step in *The Path to Smart Training Decisions* and:

■ Explain the meaning of the major question.

■ Describe appropriate and inappropriate training practices you need to look out for in assessing your options.

■ Provide you with the additional information and guidance you need to further investigate your options through general probe questions at the end of each chapter.

The Path to Smart Training Decisions flowchart and worksheet leads you to examine how a training program is or was *developed* to ensure that it includes all of the essential elements of criterion-referenced training. Why is it important to look at how training is developed? Because effective training is developed by following a systematic performance process. It is not unusual to find traditional subject matter based programs that appear to be or claim to be criterion-referenced, but are not. They may be cleverly disguised with irrelevant practice activities. A program may have performance objectives, lots of practice exercises, and require employees to master each objective. Employees may find it to be a pleasant experience. However, it lacks the cohesiveness that makes criterion-referenced programs so effective and efficient. Here are some typical "yes, but" deficiencies:

■ Yes, it has performance objectives, but they weren't derived from an analysis of a job. They were inferred after the fact from traditional subject matter resources.

■ Yes, it has practice exercises, but they are not relevant to the skills that employees need to learn and they do not include timely feedback and guidance.

■ Yes, it requires employees to master each objective, but mastery of irrelevant skills is not equivalent to job competence.

■ Yes, it provides employees with fun activities that are enjoyable, but it does not provide them with useful skills.

As you'll see as you go through *The Path to Smart Training Decisions*, many programs may look like the real thing, but aren't at all. You have to take the pig out of the poke to see how it grew up—how it was developed. You have to ask questions and know how to interpret the answers you hear.

The Path to
Smart Training Decisions

*Follow along on The Path to Smart Training Decisions
flowchart and worksheet as you go through the steps.*

Chapter 2

IS THERE A BUSINESS NEED? Is there a substantial need for training?

Is There a Business Need?

Is training done only because of a policy that every employee must receive training whether he or she needs it or not? Or is training done in response to corporate needs? This is a critical distinction. If training is done only for its own sake, both internal customers and upper management will see it largely as a drain on the budget and as diverting valued employees from their jobs. If training is done in response to corporate needs, internal customers and upper management will see training as a necessary and valued tool for maintaining and improving corporate operations.

Would you prefer to count "warm bodies" or "needs met"? How do you want training to be seen in your corporation? Clearly, you want to be valued by those around you. Make sure that you can identify and justify a business need for every training project you consider undertaking.

How Training Projects Are Initiated

The initiation of a new training project can come about in three ways:

1. You are asked to determine what training is needed to support an identified business need and to provide that training.

2. You identify a proposed or ongoing business need and undertake to determine what training is required.

3. You receive a request for training or a solicitation to provide training, and you must determine whether there is a business need.

In the first two conditions, you start with an identified business need which leads you to initiate a training project. At this point the project consists of an investigation to determine if there are training requirements and, if so, what they are. That's the next step in the path to smart training decisions. In the third condition, someone approaches you with a request to provide training or solicits you to buy a training program, and you must determine whether the training is justified.

Can You Justify It?

Several different kinds of business situations could create the need for training:

- Preparing replacement employees, either because of normal turnover (including promotions and reassignments) or expansion of an activity or department.

- Implementing business strategies, such as:

  - Introducing new processes such as new computer systems or total quality management procedures or partnering with customers and/or suppliers.

  - Downsizing or re-structuring, requiring the remaining employees to take on added tasks for which they are not skilled.

  - Changing management or cultural practices and processes, such as introducing self-managing work teams or empowering existing employees with greater responsibility.

- Enhancing the performance of current employees.

Ideally, all training projects should be related to one or more of these kinds of business needs. Projects should contribute to the organization's overall growth or business strategy.

I would like to tell you never to undertake training projects that do not serve a real business need. But that would not be practical or realistic. There are many significant players in and around most corporations who know little, if anything, about effective training, but believe that their experiences have made them experts. They may be managers, executives, union officials, major consultants, or external customers. They can make demands for training projects that you know do not support any business need, but which you cannot refuse simply because of their influence. And you may not have the time right now to educate them properly about training. Do what it takes for now but target those influential individuals for education about making smart training decisions in the near future.

Document It

Document the initiating condition as soon as you decide there is a business need that you must deal with. Getting this information documented in advance gives you a solid context for the training decisions you will make. Documentation is also important to establish a record of what training actions have been taken and why. Companies often continue training programs beyond the point of usefulness out of habit or because of personal interests. Instructors may want job security, employees might like the break from work, or maybe it's just that no one wants to take the initiative to end them. Often the original business need is accomplished or the need changes, but the training goes on as originally designed. Continuing training programs beyond their time is a very expensive practice for the company and also tends to erode the training department's reputation for providing good return on investment. For these reasons, it's useful to document and periodically review the business needs underlying each continuing training program. Here are the things you need to document to support your decisions as you travel down *The Path to Smart Training Decisions*.

> ■ Describe the business need. What is its importance? This could include things like what processes are affected. What will be lost if the need is not met or if the strategy fails? What will be gained if it succeeds? Is it a survival strategy? Who is the driving force behind it? Is it a corporate need, a division need, or a department need?

- Identify the job positions that are involved in the processes addressed by the business need.

- Identify the number to be trained. How many people may need training? Ten, a hundred, three hundred a year for five years?

- Document the gender mix of the employees to be trained.

- Identify the location(s) of the employees. Are they all in the same place or are they in different locations?

- Describe the general level of employees' education. Are they all high school grads? All college grads? A combination?

- Identify the primary language. Do all speak the same language?

- Document the general turnover rate.

- Describe other defining characteristics of the employees to be trained. Your description could include things like the following:

  - *What is their employment status?* Are they current employees or new hires?

  - *What is their skill status?* Are you upgrading their skills or preparing them for advancement?

  - *What is the age range?* Example: eighteen to seventy-two; forty and over; thirty and under.

  - *What is the level of reading and language skills?* Example: all are adequate readers at a tenth grade level or better; most are not native English speakers and read formal English well, but speak it poorly; most are poor readers and many are functionally illiterate.

  - *What level are their writing skills?* Example: most have difficulty constructing a simple sentence; all write well, but not in English; all are quite capable of writing a business report.

- *What is their concept of their job role?* Example: employees do what they are told to do and no more; supervisors and managers tell employees what to do; employees are ready and eager to accept more responsibility in their job roles. Do they have the attitude that it is better not to try than to try and fail, or do they believe in doing their best regardless of the career risk?

- *How willing are employees to participate in the training?* Example: unwilling to leave their jobs or their customers for more than a few hours at a time; fearful of classrooms and traditional presentation-based instruction; unwilling to expose their abilities and judgment before their colleagues or subordinates; aware of their deficiencies and willing to do whatever it takes to correct them; anxious to succeed in the company.

PROBE QUESTION

To recap, here is some guidance to ensure that training would fulfill a business need.

For Both To-Be-Developed and Existing Training Programs

1. What is the business need/issue?

Support or inquire into these kinds of responses:

- Rising sales projections mean increased production and new hires.
- Downsizing means fewer people need to do more jobs.
- New database or product will result in new procedures.
- Production errors are high compared to our competition. We suspect workers' performance errors are the cause.

Reject or be skeptical about these kinds of responses:

- "The Twelve Habits of Creative Time Management for Empowered Workers with Right Brains" is really popular right now. We don't want our people to be the last to get this.
- I've got to get some of these people out of here while we get organized, so I'm sending then to training.

- Some of the people in this department haven't been through training in over a year, so we need to get them into a program.
- Our high performers need a reward.

Chapter 3

STEP 2

IS THE FOCUS ON PERFORMANCE? Does the program focus on things you want trainees to *do* that they aren't able to do now?

Your Progress to this Point

■ You have identified and documented a justifiable business need for training.

Is There a *Performance* Problem?

Ask yourself what targeted employees are not *doing* now on the job that they need to do. If the answer is "Nothing," you do not need a training program. If there *is* something they are not doing, you need to ask why. Are they not doing it because they do not know how or for some other reason? A good performance consultant (there may be one right in your own training department) can help you sort out the possibilities (i.e., lack of motivation, improper equipment, etc.). If the problem exists because employees do not have the skills they need, you need training.

If the intent of the program is simply to provide people with information rather than to teach them skills to apply on the job, it is not a training program.

For example, an orientation session for new employees does not give them information they need to apply. But be careful. Sometimes trainers and instructors present information with the expectation that people will apply it in job situations. An example of this would be giving a sales force information about new products they need to sell. The expectation that employees will apply information marks the program as training. But if there *is* such an expectation, the training should do more than present the information: it also needs to provide practice in the job performances in which that information is applied. It's crucial to be able to differentiate between programs that sound like they're focused on skills and the real thing. To make sure that the program is focusing on skills and only skills, the training developer must first work to determine a list of the *tasks* that make up each job. A "task" is defined as a series of steps leading to a meaningful outcome (Mager 1997b).

Developing Task Lists

To identify the performance focus of training programs, performance technologists develop task lists. Having the training provider develop task lists is a way to ensure that the focus is on the skills you need your employees to learn. Think of it this way: suppose you had a movie camera that recorded people's thoughts and actions. Using this camera, you make a movie of everything an employee does in a particular job. Then you take the film into your cutting room and cut it into strips that show the employee doing one activity, such as:

- Diagnosing and repairing a malfunction in production machine XYZ.

- Facilitating a team meeting.

- Researching a design issue.

- Planning the development of an activity vision statement.

Each strip represents a task performed in that job, and each task has a meaningful beginning and end. We give each strip a name. The complete set of named strips comprises all the tasks that make up that person's job. Different people might cut the strips into somewhat different lengths. Some might have strips that would include two or three of another person's strips.

In the same way, task lists break performances down into smaller units of action and thought. Unfortunately, no ingenious engineer has yet invented a camera with which we can record both external and internal performances. So how does a performance technologist develop a task list? There are a number

FIGURE 3.1 TASK LIST EXAMPLES

Social and Interpersonal Tasks

Your company has developed a strategy for developing new products. All managers need to get employees' work beliefs and expectancies aligned with the new strategy, get employees to work supportively with each other, and develop a process in which employees work together to develop innovative products and services. These tasks may be briefly specified as follows:

✔ Develop a plan for modifying a group's nonsupportive beliefs and expectancies.

✔ Apply appropriate incentives to build an individual's supportive work interactions with other members of his or her work group and with other work groups.

✔ Apply appropriate incentives to increase the design of innovative products and services from individuals and groups.

These are activities each manager will need to be able to do to implement the strategy. Each one specifies a significant outcome necessary for achieving the new strategy.

Troubleshooting

Your job is to develop training for the technicians who maintain your company's production equipment. What would the task list look like? Here is a list that includes the kinds of tasks you should expect to see:

✔ Troubleshoot malfunction symptoms.

✔ Repair/replace malfunctioning components.

✔ Perform scheduled preventive maintenance activities.

✔ Tag out equipment for maintenance.

✔ Report/document maintenance activities.

✔ Plan/coordinate maintenance activities with line supervisor.

✔ Maintain spare parts inventory.

✔ Maintain maintenance tools and test instruments.

✔ Operate system/equipment.

Clearly, these items represent types of tasks, not specific tasks for any given job. For example, vibration symptoms may be broken out as a special class of troubleshooting. We may find that there are several tasks to perform to maintain each tool or test instrument.

of ways to go about it. Most technologists will use several ways in combination, depending on the job they are describing. Here are some of the more common methods:

- Have an employee describe a typical day or shift at work or keep a job diary in which he or she records everything he or she does during the day.

- Observe an employee doing various parts of the job.

- Describe the larger work processes (for example, team activities at a workstation on a production line) or events (a planned outage) to which a given job contributes. (In this way, the technologist can determine what needs to be accomplished by the job to make the larger processes or events proceed properly.)

- Review work documents and records to identify special incidents that need to be addressed.

- Identify major activities that constitute the crux of the job (for example, making a sales call, making a maintenance call at a customer's location, or preparing the work plan and budget for an activity). Then ask the employee to list the tasks that need to be accomplished before and during the activity.

- Review the job processes recommended by noted experts and shape those processes to fit a specific job.

You may need to be involved in deciding which approaches to use since it may well affect the quality and the cost of the analysis. Figure 3.1 shows examples of task lists.

Performances Versus Attributes

Typically, the process of identifying tasks can be complicated by the fact that managers' requests for training fall into two categories:

1. Worker performance: employees are either doing something they shouldn't be doing or not doing something they should be doing.

2. Worker attributes: employees are not exhibiting desirable traits or they are exhibiting undesirable traits.

But these concerns often are not judged as being different things in terms of training needs. What's the difference? And what difference does it make within a training program?

When managers specify a performance, their intent is clear. For example, an employee taking a customer's order is a performance. We know what they are talking about, and when there is a problem, we can determine whether it is a training problem. If it is, we can proceed to develop the task list and analyze those tasks to determine the skills employees need to learn.

But when managers specify *attributes*, their intent is not so clear. For example, suppose there is something your employees are not doing that you would like for them to do, but you identify it with a word or phrase such as the following:

- Be a leader when necessary.

- Work creatively.

- Work with dedication and loyalty to the company.

- Be customer service oriented.

- Be safety conscious at all times.

- Take pride in the company.

- Be a team player.

- Be an empowered worker.

That isn't a list of performances; it is a list of attributes. Employees doing different jobs in different companies may exhibit the same attribute in very different ways. Two managers' varying interpretations of the same attribute could lead to very different performance expectations for employees. If a performance need is phrased in terms of attributes, what will employees do on the job and practice during the training program? You can learn about leadership and about your own leadership styles, for example, without actually practicing any skill that would be part of leadership. If you do not actually practice the performances that make up leadership, you will not get any better at doing it, although you may get better at talking about it.

Programs on attributes commonly provide employees with simple generic exercises. The expectation is that doing the exercises will strengthen the employees' expression of the attribute in all the situations of their lives. It does not work that way. Attributes are not forces inside people that can be strengthened through exercise the way a muscle is strengthened. For instance, the practice of solving puzzles in unique ways does not make us more creative managers. It simply makes us better at solving puzzles. Attributes are descriptive terms we use to specify people's typical conduct. They are okay for use in casual conversation and gossip, but they are not useful for resolving gaps in human performance. In fact, they can be misleading.

Does this mean that upper management cannot do anything about its concerns over various attributes of employees in the corporation (leadership or loyalty, for instance)? Of course not. Rather, it means that you cannot act on management's concern until you have identified the performances that make up "leadership" (or some other attribute) in the situations that actually occur to employees in the corporation. A common way to turn vague attributes like "leadership" or "working creatively" into concrete performances is attribute analysis.

Some companies choose to describe jobs entirely in terms of attributes—that is, in terms of values, attitudes, and motives. There are many activities that might be well enhanced by these kinds of job descriptions, but training development is not among them. Many companies that use attributes to develop job descriptions don't realize that effective training cannot be built directly from those attributes. There must be an intermediate analysis in which attributes are analyzed into tasks and tasks are linked to business processes. Business processes can then be traced to business results and goals. It is probably most efficient and effective to conduct the attribute analysis and develop the job descriptions in a single, combined effort.

Attribute Analysis

To resolve attributes into performances, performance technologists use attribute analysis.[1] In cases in which problems or needs are described in terms of attributes, you must resolve the attribute into performances before you can determine whether it is a training problem and identify the skills employees will need to learn.

Suppose we wanted our employees to be good team players. The attribute analysis would proceed in two stages. In the first stage, the analyst would lead

---

1. What I am calling *attribute analysis* is the same as Robert F. Mager's *goal analysis* (1997a). It is a procedure for developing *operational definitions* for intangible human attributes; that is, defining abstract concepts in terms of the operations used to observe or measure them.

stakeholders through brainstorming the characteristics of good team players in your company's work environment. Some of the items on the list might look like this:

- Interact positively with other team members.

- Take initiative in identifying process problems.

- Complete all work assignments.

- Help others complete their work assignments.

In the second stage, the analyst would lead stakeholders through listing more specific performances for each item in the list. For instance, we might list the following performances for "Interact positively with other team members":

- Commend other team members for doing good work and for making contributions to team activities.

- Do not say demeaning or disparaging things to other team members.

- Do not use language or expressions that are offensive to other members of the team.

- Thank other team members for help or assistance.

- Listen actively to other team members' ideas and opinions about work-related issues.

- Tactfully offer other team members constructive criticism on their work and team-related activities.

Some of these performances are tasks in themselves. Some are criteria or standards for other tasks. You don't need to be concerned about what to call each performance. You just need to make sure that your list focuses on performances—and only performances.

What to Avoid: Subject Matter Programs

Instead of identifying the tasks that make up a performance, many traditional programs rely on the presentation of material related to the job at hand for students to learn how to do the job. Traditional subject matter instruction leaves it up to the student to figure out how to do this. That isn't enough; even good students don't do this well enough to apply the information on the job fully and consistently.

CRI identifies the mental skills needed to do a task. This procedure ensures that the recall of each item of information is triggered by real cues in the performance of the job at the moment it is needed.

How do you evaluate a training program that focuses on presenting information about some subject matter, such as the psychology of leadership, the sociology of teams, the philosophy of total quality management, or the theory of operation of a system? Though there is no mention of the application of the subject matter in the employees' work environments, there may be an implied application. Would your technicians be better troubleshooters if they knew more about how the equipment they maintain works? Would your salespeople better fit product features to customer needs if they knew more about the products they are selling?

This is a traditional approach to education and training: "Tell 'em about it and let them figure out what to do with it." Most employees will not figure out how to apply facts and principles learned in traditional training—or if they do figure it out, it will take a long time to apply it. This is *not* an effective approach for business use.

"But wait a minute," you say. "Technicians should know how the equipment they maintain works, and salespeople should have strong product knowledge." Of course, technicians should know how the equipment works. But how much should they know? You can put limits on how much they need to know only if you first identify how they will use the information. Here are some performances that would require technicians to have information about how a system works:

- Given a malfunction symptom, identify other symptoms whose presence needs to be determined.

- Given a symptom pattern, identify all the functional blocks that could contain the source of the malfunction.

- Given a string of suspect functional blocks, select an efficient checkpoint for narrowing the string.

- Given a string of suspect functional blocks and the outcome of a measurement or observation made at a checkpoint, identify which functional blocks are no longer suspect.

These are the kinds of performances technicians do on the job and the kinds of performances on which the training should focus. Similarly, salespeople need to practice converting new product information into customer benefits. Just being able to recite product information does not mean they will be able to apply that information effectively when the time arises.

Traditionally, efforts to increase innovation in the design of new products and services in a company would consist of lecturing managers on creativity, networking, expectancies, beliefs, and incentives, and letting them figure out how to apply this knowledge on the job to accomplish the strategy. The managers would have to transform a complex body of knowledge into practical actions, but without the necessary time, the resources, or the training and experience. There is little chance that many of them would succeed. The strategy would fail.

Subject Matter Signs: "Information Overload"

When a program claims that procedures are built into the program to prevent "information overload," this is a clear giveaway that it is a subject matter program rather than one based on performance. The procedures for preventing information overload sound sensible—break the presentations down into manageable "chunks," build in lots of activities (not necessarily relevant to the job), provide graphics to illustrate concepts, use memory devices, organize content around principles, and so forth. The first two procedures, however, should not even be necessary. CRI uses task analysis (discussed in step 3) to automatically break practice into manageable chunks and mental components around job relevant activities. The remaining procedures are simply good instructional practices to use whenever appropriate.

Information overload procedures do help employees learn overwhelming amounts of information—whether they need it or not. However, these procedures still do not provide employees with guidance on how to sort out relevant information from irrelevant or how to apply that information on the job.

Watching for "Hidden" Performances in Instruction

What people do on the job is not just what we see them do. It also includes those things we cannot see but which they experience—perceptions, mental activities (self-talk and imagery), and feelings. Whatever employees do in a training program is what they learn. If they daydream about being elsewhere or ruminate about how much they hate being in the class and how boring the instructor is, that is what they will learn. If they practice doing those things they need to do on the job, then that's what they will learn. Obviously, you want your employees to practice all of the things that are relevant to the job they are learning.

Hidden performances most commonly arise from old subject matter habits of thought. Old habits of thought can lead us into continuing to believe that if we give employees information we think they need, they will be able to apply it. Here are some examples.

■ New product knowledge training for sales reps: Do we just tell them the features of the new product, or do we also give them practice converting those features to customer benefits? The latter leads to far more successful new product roll-outs, even though reps have been applying this skill with other products for years.

■ Safety navigation in a dangerous work area or during emergency conditions in an ordinary work area: Do we just tell them where the safe paths are (show them a map), or do we walk them through the paths as they explain the dangers to us? Again, the latter leads to far more effective safety practices in a workforce than the former.

■ New hire training: Do we just tell them about their benefit options and how to get things done in the company? They may need coaching through some benefit decisions. Walking them through critical action processes in the company may make them productive much sooner than letting them bumble through on their own.

Hidden performances may also lurk in our common use of attribute and trait words to describe the people with whom we interact. For example, management may want employees to be "a little sharper." "A little sharper" is an attribute even though management may not recognize it as such.

PROBE QUESTIONS

To recap, here are some questions to ensure that the proposed training program focuses on the necessary job performances.

For Both To-Be-Developed and Existing Training Programs

1. What are our employees not accomplishing now that they ought to be accomplishing?

Support or inquire into these kinds of responses:

• They are new hires who have had experience in other companies but don't know our procedures.

- The new product contains some new technology requiring new skills for both operation and maintenance.
- Workers are mishandling delicate electronic components that change the adjustments made earlier in the process. (*This could be a performance problem or a process problem, but it needs to be investigated.*)

Reject or be skeptical about these kinds of responses:

- They need to learn basic theories of management/leadership/ how to avoid sexual harassment. (*These are worthwhile issues, but they need to be defined in terms of performances.*)

2. What skills are they missing that prevent them from accomplishing what they ought to accomplish?

Support or inquire into these kinds of responses:

- They need to learn how we assign jobs, how to fill out reports, how to get spare parts, how to keep their trucks ready, and so on. But once they get to the job, they are already able to fix the equipment.
- Mechanics have to learn how to do easy fixes on computers, and electronic techs need to learn how to do easy mechanical fixes.

3. To ensure that the new skills are applied effectively on the job, what else will we need to do? For example, will we need to train or retrain supervisors, managers, or colleagues? Will we need to revise personnel policies, production policies, incentives, job aids, procedures?

Support or inquire into these kinds of responses:

- We will conduct a series of meetings with supervisors and managers to explain the business strategy addressed by the training, to determine what other actions are needed, and to get input for the planning and development of those actions.

For Existing Training Programs

1. Do the performance objectives of the program specify the skills employees need?

Support or inquire into these kinds of responses:

- These objectives cover all the same tasks and skills our

people perform in very similar conditions.

- This is off-the-shelf training from a vendor, but the objectives require employees to apply the skills in their own situations during practice.

Reject or be skeptical about these kinds of responses:

- This is a quality coaching program developed for one of the world's leading investment houses. Sure, we are a production company, but coaching is coaching. (*No it isn't. It's somewhat different with different people in different circumstances.*)

2. Were the performance objectives derived from similar jobs performed by similar employees in similar work situations?

Support or inquire into these kinds of responses:

- This program was developed for linemen in another power company operating in the same general environment and climate as we do.

Chapter 4

STEP 3 **ARE TASKS AND SKILLS DETAILED?** Have or will the specific job tasks and skills be named and described in detail?

Your Progress to This Point

- ■ You have identified and documented a justifiable business need.

- ■ You have established that the program will focus specifically on the things employees need to learn.

Now you have to be sure that the emerging program will focus on the specific performances that are creating difficulties for your employees in the situations that arise in their jobs. Sometimes programs are focused on performance, but fail to focus on all the *right* performances.

Why does it matter if training is focused on all the right performances? Practice during training builds the connections that drive performance on the job later. Wrong practice means those neural connections won't be made, and performance will have to be corrected through job experience. The problem with this is that job experience is not nearly as effective or efficient as practice in training because it occurs by chance, without the coaching, guidance, and feedback available in training. Learning through experience is a very iffy proposition. If practice has enforced the wrong habits, it may actually interfere with learning correct performances by means of job experience later—a "double whammy." Undoing the damage that has been done is oftentimes much more difficult than learning by experience alone.

Avoiding the Wrong Kind of Performance

Many off-the-shelf training programs focus on tasks, but the tasks are generic tasks in generic situations. In generic practice, the tasks and skills specific to the job at hand have not been detailed. Generic tasks often omit the steps found in specific applications, such as judgments about conditions, shortcuts, availability of tools, and so on. While not necessarily bad for initial learning, if that's all the learning focuses on, then you have a problem. There are not many generic workers doing generic tasks in generic companies. As discussed in chapter 1, learning consists of assembling neurons into neural circuits. Generic tasks form some of the right connections, but rarely enough to trigger the right perceptions and performances in the job environment. Graduates of such programs still have a lot of dots to connect all on their own and will not be up to speed at graduation. Many of them never will take the trouble to do the additional figuring and practice that they need to apply information on the job. For generic practice to be useful, it has to lead to realistic practice, in which employees practice their own specific tasks in their own work environments—or simulations of them—before the training ends.

If you are considering a program that contains only generic practice, try to supplement it with realistic practice in realistic job contexts. Preferably, the program should have supplementary practice integrated throughout rather than added as a separate unit after the completion of the program.

Unidentified Mental Skills: "Theory in the Morning, Lab in the Afternoon"

If the program you are considering teaches "theory in the morning, lab in the afternoon" or a variation of this, this is a sign that you need to ask some penetrating questions. This is a form of training that mixes performance and subject matter approaches. The lab section usually provides employees with performance instruction, while the theory section often consists of lectures on related and unrelated topics. Separate instructors may even teach the two sections, each going his or her own way.

The primary problem with this approach is that the mental components (or skills) of complex performances are not identified. Theory presentations in which mental skills haven't been identified by the program designers can overwhelm students with relevant and irrelevant information mixed together. Students receive little or no guidance on how to sort relevant from irrelevant or how to apply the relevant information in a work environment. The mental performances that employees need to learn are often either omitted or lost. For instance, if employees are learning to troubleshoot a system that does not have diagnostics built into it, they need to be able to:

■ Trace and describe flow through the functional components that produce the system's outputs from the outputs back to the inputs.

■ Select, make, and interpret various control settings or checkpoint measurements so that they can narrow the initial list of suspect components.

These are the kinds of mental skills employees should learn in the program. Even mental skills are characterized by active verbiage—employees can demonstrate performances like tracing or selecting and instructors can verify their competence. The verbs "to know" and "to understand" are passive and are not acceptable. In theory/lab courses, however, employees usually get a lot of content characterized by passive terminology and subject matter and topic nouns: "know Ohm's Law," "understand electron flow," and so on. It is left to employees to weed through the information and organize it in a way that makes it useful in the act of troubleshooting. The course designers should be the ones organizing the information, as well as describing the mental skills with active verbs.

The Steps to Focusing on the Right Performances

You want employees to learn in class what you want them to do on the job. You want them to practice all the skills they need to perform the job tasks in realistic work situations. To determine what skills and in what situations your employees will need to practice, training developers must analyze the jobs into tasks and skills. The information you obtain can be used to build a training program or to customize an existing generic program with supplementary practice.

The analysis also must identify the mental components of job performances. The employees need to practice the mental skills just as they practice any other skill. Many of these mental skills comprise the theory employees actually need to learn. In criterion-referenced programs, this theory will be presented in bits and pieces scattered throughout the program in the performance contexts in which they occur on the job, rather than as large blocks of information (as usually found in subject matter programs).

Finding the Right Performances: Task Analysis

The performances that the training program ultimately addresses are initially identified by means of task analysis. The task analysis is a step-by-step description of how a piece of the job is done. It describes the actual job that the employees will be trained to perform. From the results of the task analysis, the training developer will be able to infer the skills—perceptual, manual, and mental—that will be taught and practiced in the training program. Figure 4.1 shows a sample task analysis for troubleshooting. The steps in the flowchart include both physical and mental activities. Notice how the flowchart contains a large feedback loop that describes steps that are repeated until only one suspect source remains. This is one of the advantages of flowcharting tasks. The flowchart makes repeated steps much more visible.

The performance technologists responsible for doing task analysis will need substantial access to several exemplary job performers from your corporation. These exemplary performers must be familiar with the job environment and with the characteristics of those who will be trained. Above all, they must be people who have the patience to explain what they do to someone who may know absolutely nothing about their job. The performance technologists and the exemplary job performers will identify all the tasks to be addressed by the training (see step 2). Then they will develop the detailed description, usually a flowchart, for performing each task (including its mental components). The result of the task analysis is task steps. From those task steps, the training developer can infer the skills your employees need to practice, which we'll talk about in a moment. First though, some training developers might stop at tasks and use them as the smallest unit of practice. That isn't necessarily the best route if you want your training program to be as efficient as possible.

The Advantage of a Skill-Based Approach to Training

One of the more common approaches to performance instruction is to have employees practice entire tasks as the smallest unit of practice (task-based approach). A much better approach also breaks tasks into smaller skills and designs practice around both (skill-based approach). Though a task-based training approach is better than a traditional subject matter approach, it is not nearly as efficient as a skill-based approach. The skill-based approach is a more

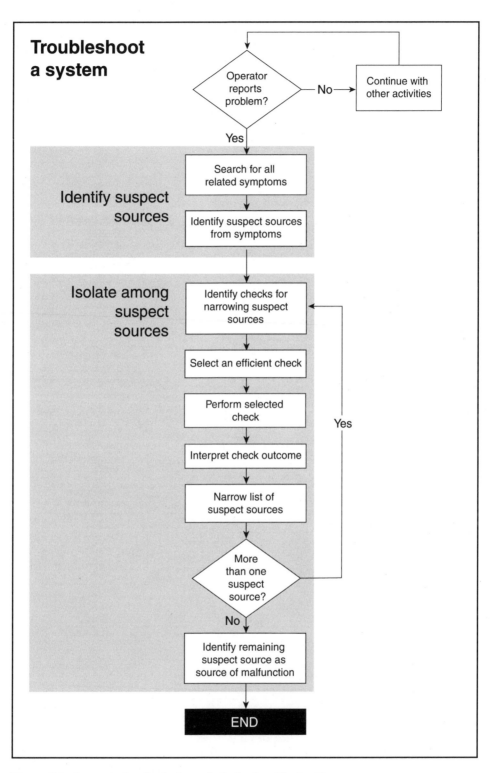

Figure 4-1. An example of a task analysis for troubleshooting

Are Tasks and Skills Detailed?

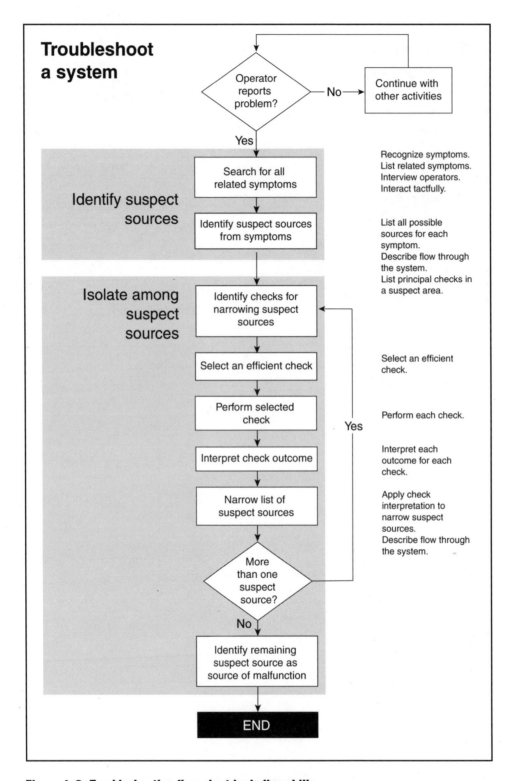

Troubleshoot a system

Operator reports problem? — No → Continue with other activities

Yes

Identify suspect sources

Search for all related symptoms

Identify suspect sources from symptoms

Recognize symptoms.
List related symptoms.
Interview operators.
Interact tactfully.

List all possible sources for each symptom.
Describe flow through the system.
List principal checks in a suspect area.

Isolate among suspect sources

Identify checks for narrowing suspect sources

Select an efficient check

Perform selected check

Interpret check outcome

Narrow list of suspect sources

More than one suspect source?

Yes

Select an efficient check.

Perform each check.

Interpret each outcome for each check.

Apply check interpretation to narrow suspect sources.
Describe flow through the system.

No

Identify remaining suspect source as source of malfunction

END

Figure 4–2. Troubleshooting flow chart including skills.

efficient way of providing practice to employees. It provides special practice conditions for common components of performance and excludes components the employee may already have mastered.

Let's take another look at the troubleshooting example. Figure 4.2 shows the same flowchart but also includes the skills that are part of each step in the flowchart. If an employee practices only complete troubleshooting *tasks*, it will take many practice trials to learn to troubleshoot. Every practice trial will require the employee to go through all the steps in the task. However, if practice is first provided on each of the *skills* to job competence, the entire task will need far fewer practice trials. Some skills will require many practice trials (for instance, "List all probable sources for each symptom"), and others will require much less practice (for instance, "Perform each check"). Since the skills are smaller than the overall task, more practice trials can be given to the difficult skills than would otherwise be possible in the same amount of time. The reduction in practice time on easier skills more than makes up for the added time on more difficult skills. This form of practice is more efficient and focused on each employee's needs.

The relationships among the tasks and skills in a skill-based approach are usually shown in clusters of skill hierarchies (Mager and Pipe 1994). Figure 4.3 shows a sample skill hierarchy for the skills derived from our troubleshooting example.

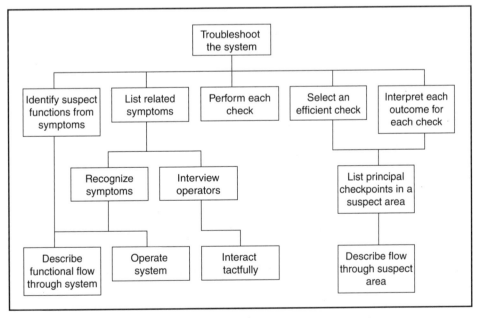

Figure 4–3. Skill hierarchy for a troubleshooting task.

Are Tasks and Skills Detailed?

Learning is more efficient if the lower skills are learned before the higher skills to which they are connected by a line. On the right side of the hierarchy are skills that technicians who are experienced in maintaining similar systems already possess. If you were developing a program intended to upgrade experienced technicians, you could omit these skills. In a program for both experienced and inexperienced technicians, technicians could test out of those skills. Skill hierarchies allow much more flexibility in the design of training programs and help make training more useful and efficient. Why should you care about training efficiency? The less efficient the training, the longer your employees will be off the job. If you have several hundred to several thousand employees to train, even short delays can be costly.

Ask your training sources to show you samples of previous skill hierarchies they have developed and have them explain their work to you. They should include specific mental skills (not big chunks of content) as well as explicit action skills. The hierarchy should have mental skills distributed throughout it and not all clustered in one place.

The Next Step: Inferring Skills

Some training developers identify skills by asking job incumbents what skills are needed to do the job or some tasks from the job. They may say, "We pulled some expert performers for a couple of days and got their input on the skills it takes to do this job." This alone is not a satisfactory procedure. Exemplary performers are not good sources for identifying skills because they are likely to make two kinds of errors:

1. They will make "knowledge" statements that are too broad rather than specific performance statements. ("They need to know how it works" versus "They need to be able to trace flow on this level of diagram.")

2. They will fail to mention critical skills that are so ingrained in their own performance that they fail to recognize them as skills.

How do we get around this problem? The training developer infers the skills, but after developing a task description with the expert performer's input. And, of course, the training developer will have the expert performer verify the skills. The training developer creates the description based on input from the performers, and it is complete once the exemplary performers verify it as the correct procedure.

You want to see each link in a clear chain of logic from job to task, task to task step, task step to skill, skill to practice exercise, and from practice to verification of job competence. You want to see specific mental skills (that is, mental activities) rather than broad "knowledges." Here are some examples from the previous troubleshooting skill hierarchy (see figure 4.3):

- Describe functional flow through the system.

- Recognize symptoms.

- Identify suspect functions from symptoms.

- List related symptoms.

- Interpret each outcome for each check.

These skills all contain active verbs, and they are *mental* skills. A skill such as "Apply electronic theory" does not tell the developer what specifically to do to perform the task or skill. The skills listed in the bullets above do help the developer perform the task. The training developer has to push the exemplary performers until they are able to produce a complete set of statements for each task step. The exemplary performers are the final judges regarding the content of each statement, but the training developers are the final judges on the quality of each statement.

Questionnaire-Based Task Analysis

Avoid questionnaire-based task analysis. It consists of having just about everyone who currently does the job and their supervisors respond to questionnaires prepared by the developers. These questionnaires identify the tasks performed at the various job locations and the characteristics of those tasks, particularly frequency of occurrence and difficulty. This procedure provides little useful information for training development and is quite expensive. It characterizes the tasks, but it does not detail them. It is often used to eliminate non-critical, infrequent, or easy tasks from inclusion in the training program.

When time allows, such decisions are better made at the skill level with skill hierarchies. When time does not allow, then this kind of information can be used to eliminate tasks before analyzing them so that the effort can focus on the more productive tasks. Even in these applications, however, it is not necessary to collect information from a large sample of respondents. One or two carefully selected respondents from each significant work location is usually sufficient.

PROBE QUESTIONS

To recap, here are some questions to ensure specific job tasks are named and described in detail.

For To-Be-Developed Training Programs

1. From what sources of information will the task list be developed? Will the tasks be aligned with the requirements of larger corporate processes?

    Support or inquire into these kinds of responses:

    *   We are not changing the job, so we can involve exemplary performers as sources and co-analysts. We will review documentation and incident records on the job. We will interview a sample of managers and supervisors.

    *   This is a new job, so we will interview those people closest to it to determine the kinds of situations in which the job will be done. We will gather information about the job functions and tasks from engineers, experts, books and papers, and equipment documentation. We will involve members of the target population as co-analysts. And, finally, we will conduct limited tests of crucial tasks to make sure the procedures we have developed work.

    Reject or be skeptical about these kinds of responses:

    *   We are not changing the job, so we will ask managers to release one or two employees who currently do the job to be our sources of information. (*They need to be exemplary performers, they need to be volunteers, and never trust a manager or supervisor to release one of his or her best workers. They are much more likely to release someone they can well do without.*)

    *   This is a new job. Our information source will be an outside consultant who has done this job in another company. (*You also need information on the situations and conditions in which the job will be done in this company and on the people who will do it. And you need to make sure the procedures you describe will actually work before you build the training program.*)

2. What role will exemplary job performers play in making judgments about how the job is or will be performed?

Reject or be skeptical about these kinds of responses:

- The analysts are expert in doing this job in other locations, and they will derive the skills. We won't have to pull your people off their jobs at all.

3. How will the job information be obtained?

Support or inquire into these kinds of responses:

- Personal contact in face-to-face, telephone, or e-mail (in that order) interviews with exemplary performers.

Reject or be skeptical about these kinds of responses:

- Mail-out questionnaires to as many job holders in the company as possible. (*This format can be insensitive to the type of information really needed for training development. It generates impressive numbers but little useful information.*)

For Existing Training Programs

1. Are tasks specific to your employees' jobs included in the program?

Support or inquire into these kinds of responses:

- The program has generic tasks and skills in early practice, but later practice is always concerned with the participants' own tasks and skills which they bring with them.

Reject or be skeptical about these kinds of responses:

- The tasks and skills in the program have been culled from far ranging analyses in many companies to represent the most typical and critical work situations that are encountered. We offer the broadest knowledge base for our training programs in the industry.

2. Are the principal applications derived from one or more case studies taken from other organizations? Can ones taken from your organization's conditions and requirements replace them?

Support or inquire into these kinds of responses:

- Yes. We will modify or replace all the case studies to reflect your organization's conditions and requirements.

Reject or be skeptical about these kinds of responses:

- No. Our case studies have been very carefully designed to provide the best illustrations and practice for students.

3. Are there large blocks of information presented to the employees in theory or lecture units?

Reject or be skeptical of these instructional practices.

- There is little that can be done to fix such programs in the short run. It will confuse more than it will help your employees and it will damage the self-confidence of many of them. This kind of program should be totally redesigned if it is to be reliably effective and efficient. Much of the content may well be cut and pasted into the redesigned program, but in much smaller pieces scattered throughout the program.

Chapter 5

STEP 4 **IS PRACTICE REALISTIC?** Will employees practice the job skills they need to learn in realistic job contexts?

Your Progress to This Point

- You have identified and documented a justifiable business need.

- You have established that the program will focus specifically on the skills employees need to learn.

- You have ensured that the specific job tasks and skills will be named and described in detail.

So far, the development of a training program is concerned solely with determining the pieces of job performance (tasks and skills) that the employees need to learn. Each practice unit in the training program focuses on just one task or skill, leading the employees through practice and providing them with appropriate feedback and guidance.

Now you want to be sure that the employees will practice the skills they need to learn in a realistic format—that is, as it is done on the job. Without practice, little learning happens. Remember though, that if all of that practice is generic, you have a problem. This applies to the conditions in which the skills and tasks are practiced as well as to the actual actions.

Shaping Cues in Performance Situations

Two kinds of cues make up a job performance situation: triggering cues and shaping cues. Triggering cues, which we'll discuss in the next chapter, tell the employee when to initiate performance of the task or skill. Shaping cues determine the form and substance of the performance, or how it is done. It does not make any difference whether we are describing a lathe operator, a middle manager, or the CEO. The lathe operator receives signals about the setup and operation of his or her lathe. The middle manager receives signals about team operation and the effectiveness of his or her processes. The CEO receives signals about market conditions and the emerging technologies relevant to the business. Any job can be described in this manner.

For example, in order to lead a group problem solving session, an employee needs a group of people to lead plus whatever facilities and paraphernalia are needed to conduct the session. The people generate shaping cues by what they say and do during the session. A doctor performing surgery on a patient would need to respond to shaping cues in the patient's ongoing condition, such as heart rate and blood pressure.

The performer must be able to adjust his or her performance depending on the shaping cues encountered. The employee will not be successful if his or her response is not appropriate. Every job performance consists of a performer responding to signals from one or more job situations.

The Design of Practice Situations

Now that we know what shaping cues are, we are ready to review the design of the practice situations for each skill. Remember our strategy: the practice should lead the employee to do the things he needs to learn to do by presenting him with a series of messages or cues. Clearly, the practice situations have to include the performance situations found on the job. If the practice is not in a realistic job situation, the employee will not be presented with the necessary shaping cues.

Practice should be designed for each and every task and skill that employees will learn in the program. Each practice unit should lead the employees through performing the task or skill specified in the objective for that unit. The messages that lead the employees through performing each task or skill can consist of demonstrations or verbal instructions. They can be delivered before practice actually begins, in which case the employees may learn to guide their own practice by means of self-instruction. They may be delivered one at a time to guide each step during practice. Or they may be intermixed in layers. No matter how the instructions are presented, they lead the employees through the performances specified in the objectives, and the objectives, in turn, specify the performances that actually occur on the job.

Effective practice is more than just doing something over and over again. The neural circuits needed to drive each performance must be assembled into wholes from sensory input, thoughts and actions. Effective practice has to include assessment of each practice trial, timely and informative feedback, and corrective guidance.[1] The source of feedback and its manner of delivery must be appropriate to the performance and employees. Sometimes it only needs to be a predetermined answer to a practice problem given in print to the employee. At other times it may need to be a judgment made by an expert accompanied by guidance from an insightful coach. The design of each practice session must include specifications of how the employee's performance will be assessed, what kind of feedback and guidance will be needed, and how they will be delivered.

Designing practice situations is the most time-consuming phase in the development of a performance training program. Do not let developers short-cut the process by giving you practice situations that are not derived from analyses of specific jobs in your corporation. Anything less will leave dots unconnected during training. Dots not connected in training will have to be connected later on the job. That means a high risk of performance errors and learning delays—or perhaps never learning at all.

As you can see, this approach to the design of an instructional unit involves a lot more than just putting an entertaining lecture with fun and games together. Make sure this approach, or something similar to it, is used in developing the training you buy if you want a training program that works.

---

1. For more information on the components of relevant practice, see chapter 12 in Robert F. Mager's *Making Instruction Work* (1997b).

PROBE QUESTIONS

To recap, here are questions to ensure employees will practice in realistic job situations and with appropriate feedback and guidance.

For To-Be-Developed Training Programs

1. Will employees actually practice each skill and task during the program?

    Reject or be skeptical about these kinds of responses:

    *   All employees practice the major skills and tasks. On the remaining tasks and skills, one employee will actually practice the skill while the others watch. They will take turns as they move on to other skills. (*Will they also take turns doing the tasks and skills on the job?*)

2. How will employees be provided with feedback and guidance on their practice exercises?

    Reject or be skeptical about these kinds of responses:

    *   Feedback and guidance will be provided either on paper or via computer. (*This may be okay, if all practice problems lead to a hard and fast answer. But if they require expert interpretation or an observer to note what happened, then it is not okay.*)

For Existing Training Programs

1. Ask to see the employee practice exercises. Do they look like they were developed from the job or from a textbook?

    Support or inquire into these kinds of responses:

    *   All practice exercises consist of real job performances.

    Reject or be skeptical about these kinds of responses:

    *   Practice exercises have been added for every objective to ensure full understanding by the students.

2. How are employees provided with feedback and guidance in the practice exercises?

    Support or inquire into these kinds of responses:

    *   The employee receives feedback immediately after each practice exercise, either from the materials, a colleague with a check sheet, or the instructor.

Reject or be skeptical about these kinds of responses:

- Feedback is given after each block of practice exercises.
- The instructor goes over the practice exercises each night and provides feedback the following day.

Chapter 6

DOES PRACTICE INCLUDE A MIX OF JOB SITUATIONS? Is practice provided in a representative mix of job situations?

Your Progress to This Point

- You have identified and documented a justifiable business need for training.

- You have established that the program will focus specifically on the skills employees need to learn.

- You have ensured that specific tasks and skills will be named and described in detail.

- You have ensured that employees will be provided with relevant practice in realistic job formats.

Now you need to ensure that employees will practice each new skill in a representative range of job situations that will generate the appropriate *triggering cues*. Let's look at why that's so important and how you achieve it.

What Triggers Performance?

Suppose we teach a medical student the skills needed to do a routine appendectomy—and that's all. We do not teach him how to recognize appendicitis in all its appearances, and we do not teach him how to recognize the signs of a ruptured appendix. Are we ready to turn him loose on the world to practice medicine? In his present state, he will miss opportunities, he will pass others by, and he will botch others. Would you select him to be your family's physician?

Probably not. Practice that includes appropriate shaping cues generates the right employee performance on the job later. But practice also needs to build connections between the performance and the environmental conditions that trigger it—especially the more common and critical ones.

If the necessary job performances are going to occur on the job in the appropriate situations, something in the job situations has to trigger them, and employees have to recognize that trigger. Figure 6.1 shows some examples of tasks and the cues that would trigger them.

Figure 6.1

TASK: Deal with an irate customer
Triggering cue—Angry words or behavior of irate customer

TASK: Troubleshoot and repair a machine
Triggering cue—Specific malfunction symptoms

TASK: Perform a medical test on a patient
Triggering cue—Symptoms of a specific illness

These cues must be included in practice if they are to become effective triggers for the tasks being learned. Let's look at an example where triggering rarely happens.

Students in traditional schools are generally taught advanced algebra without any reference to its application in practical life situations. Consequently, many learn algebra well enough to pass the course, but have little notion of when to use what they have learned. My psychometrics professor told us of his wife's application of algebra to determine the number of pleats and their dimensions to put in a pleated skirt of a given waist size. She used simultaneous equations in three unknowns to work out her answer. Then she made the skirt. I am sure many people did well in advanced algebra but never thought to use it in designing their clothes. Why not? Because they never practiced applying advanced algebra to practical life situations.

Cognitive scientists refer to knowledge we learn but never use as *inert knowledge*. Most of what we learn in school winds up being inert knowledge. We need to avoid inert knowledge in business training. Inert knowledge in the business world costs a great deal in wasted employee time, confusion, and frustration, and is of no value to the company.

Two strategies help to avoid inert knowledge:

1. Identify all and only those performances and skills required to be effective on the job.

2. Ensure that those skills are practiced in a representative range of job situations and contexts.

By this point in your decision process, you have already ensured that the proper analysis will be conducted to focus the training on needed skills only. Now you need to ensure that the skills will be applied in the right combination in all of the appropriate job situations.

Recognizing the Skills Required: Skill Clusters

Tasks are made up of skills, but not necessarily the exact same skills every time. There may be some core skills that are involved in every performance, but others may vary depending on the situation. It is not necessary for employees to practice every single variation of a given task if they have learned all the skills and practiced them in a representative sample of the task variations. The entire set of skills that could be involved in all possible variations of a task are the task's *skill cluster*. There are three possible conditions you need to consider:

1. One skill cluster in a single situation.

2. One skill cluster in different situations.

3. Different skill clusters in different situations.

Let's examine each of these conditions and see how you handle each one.

One Skill Cluster in a Single Situation

This one is easy—or so we sometimes think. The same initiating elements trigger the appropriate performances every time they are needed on the job. So all you have to do is make sure that the same triggering and shaping cues are included in every practice trial.

Suppose you wanted your sales associates to fill out a simple form on each customer that came in your stores—name, address, and phone number. It seems so simple that training is not needed. However, that is not necessarily so. Suppose the customer just came in to look without buying anything. Do you want the associate to query the customer to fill out the form anyway? Suppose the customer says, "It's none of your business." Do you want the associate to insist? You may be able to resolve these issues simply with some straightforward policies. Instead, you may decide that you want your sales associates to push gently for the information without offending the customer. "Pushing gently without offending" is not a simple skill that everyone already possesses.

One Skill Cluster in Different Situations

In this condition, the same basic skills are used every time, but the situations in which they are used may vary considerably. Common examples of this condition are programs that teach skills for using common hand tools. Socket wrenches, open end wrenches, box wrenches, screwdrivers, and vise grips can all be used in a great variety of situations in automotive maintenance, machine repair, house construction, motorcycle repair, landscaping construction, watch repair, jewelry-making, appliance installation and repair, etc. If you are designing a course that includes teaching tool-using skills, you will need to provide practice in a representative sample of those situations that occur on the job.

Different classes of situations are often important for programs teaching equipment repair skills. The critical skills may remain the same from one situation to another, but they may take a different form in different situations. For example, it's one thing to work on new equipment in spacious, well-lighted surroundings and quite another to work on old, dirty equipment in some small, dark place with junk stacked up all around it while roaches and rats run hither and yon. Getting access to and seeing inside various parts of the equipment may be difficult and tiring in the second instance. If employees practice only in a spacious, well-lit laboratory during training, they will be ill-prepared to provide the quality service demanded by a longtime customer who has not yet upgraded his facility.

Different Skill Clusters in Different Situations

In this condition, a core of common skills is applied in every situation, and then other skills apply for some situations but not others. Common examples are programs that teach sales reps how to make sales calls on customers with different characteristics. There could be established, new, or prospective customers. Some know precisely what they want; others need to be led through a problem-solving process. Some are angry over a faulty product or over poor service in the past. Some are specifically angry at the rep. Some will pay the stated price, whatever it is. Others will negotiate for the best possible price and will challenge the rep to meet or beat quotes they have received from other companies. The different skill clusters associated with these various situations can be characterized by the theme of the situations. For example, the program might consist of different practice units for different situations with the following titles:

1. Landing the new customer

2. Caring for the happy customer

3. Calming the angry customer

4. Negotiating with the finagling customer

There may be a common skill cluster used in all of these situations and a unique skill cluster for each situation. In addition, the skill clusters for some situations may build additively from one to the other.

Situations	Skill Clusters
Landing the new customer	A
Caring for the happy customer	A + B
Calming the angry customer	A + B + C
Negotiating with the finagling customer	A + C

Troubleshooting complex equipment or complex business systems may also exhibit the same kinds of relationships between situations and skill clusters. The basic troubleshooting strategy is the same for many equipment situations. However, the implementation of that strategy may be modified for different kinds of equipment. For example, in troubleshooting electromechanical equipment, such as home appliances, after the malfunction has been isolated on the basis of the symptoms, the next step is to determine whether the malfunction is electrical or mechanical rather than dealing with both as a single, integrated system.

Prioritize the job situations in terms of their value to the company. Note the skills clusters involved in each situation. Start with the lowest priority. What skill clusters needed for the lowest priority situation can you delete without severely degrading higher priority situations? For instance, suppose the situations in the preceding example are listed in order of value to the company. The lowest priority situation requires skill clusters A and C. You can't delete A because it is required by every one of the other situations. If you delete skill cluster C, however, the two highest priority situations will not be affected and the remaining lower priority situations will be degraded but not eliminated. If you have a long list of situations involving a wide variety of skill clusters, you will probably be able to develop several different strategies for cutting costs. Present whatever strategies you develop (one or more) to management. Explain that these strategies are business strategies since they specify job responsibilities. As such, the choice among them must be made by management. And the consequences of that choice must be borne by management.

The Cost of Cutting Costs

If you wanted to cut training costs by reducing practice, then which situations would you cut from our examples? In which situations can your company afford to have its employees bumbling and fumbling for a considerable period of time as they try to figure out what to do? In which situations will your customers tolerate poor to disastrous performance from your employees? If your employees do not practice in the right situations during training, they will not make the right connections to generate effective performances on the job.

You know what the game is and the cost of losing. Find out how your training source intends to make sure all the right job situations are included in the training program.

PROBE QUESTIONS

To recap, here are questions to ensure that practice is provided in a representative mix of job situations.

For To-Be-Developed Training Programs

1. From what sources of information will the job situations be developed for practice? Will they be derived in part from larger corporate processes, such as scheduled outages as part of the preventive maintenance process?

Support or inquire into these kinds of responses:

- We will identify the most experienced employees currently in the job, form them into small groups, and have them identify and describe the most common and the most critical situations that arise on the job.

Reject or be skeptical about these kinds of responses:

- We have identified the most common situations from leading books and trade journals.

2. Is a representative sample of job performers located in a representative array of job environments among the information sources listed?

   Support or inquire into these kinds of responses:

   - Our analysts will interview employees in each region to make sure we identify all the significant job situations.

   Reject or be skeptical about these kinds of responses:

   - The region closest to us has a representative sampling of the major job responsibilities, so we will do all our interviewing there to save travel dollars.

3. How will the job information be obtained?

   Support or inquire into these kinds of responses:

   - We are going to review incident records and do small group interviews at each location we visit.

   Reject or be skeptical about these kinds of responses:

   - A twenty-page questionnaire with rating scales for each task will be mailed to everyone currently doing the job. (*Live interactions are better than paper and pencil questionnaires. Small group interviews are not only efficient, but in the hands of a skilled facilitator, they can be a productive way of acquiring valid information.*)

For Existing Training Programs

1. How readily can job situations from our organization be incorporated into the existing program? Can they be distributed appropriately throughout the program?

   - If they can, ask the questions above for to-be-developed training programs.

Chapter 7

DO LEARNERS PRACTICE TO JOB COMPETENCE? Will each employee's job competence in each skill be verified during the program?

Your Progress to This Point

- You have identified and documented a justifiable business need.

- You have established that the program will focus specifically on the skills employees need to learn.

- You have ensured that the specific job tasks involved in these performances will be named and described in detail.

- You have ensured that employees will be provided with relevant practice in realistic job formats.

- You have established that practice will be provided in a representative mix of job situations.

Now you need to establish how employee success will be determined in each practice unit (or module) and in the program.

The Measure of Success

If employee learning is going to be measured and evaluated, we have to have tests and grades, right? Wrong. While that may be how schools do it, business has different interests.

Suppose we use multiple-choice, fill-in-the-blank, true-false, and short answer test items. What do these kinds of test items tell us about whether our employees can do specific performances? They do not tell us much at all. Certainly, there is some overlap, but learning to answer these kinds of questions is not the same as learning to do the real job performances. I can describe a brain operation, but I doubt that you would want me to perform brain surgery on you.

To determine how well an employee can perform the tasks and skills required on a job, you will need to observe the employee actually performing those tasks and skills. There simply is no valid alternative. Figure 7.1 shows some examples:

Figure 7.1

TASK: Welding
Required Performance—Make three welds of the same kind as occur on the job. Performance and product must meet job standards.

TASK: Interviewing applicants
Required Performance—Interview a simulated applicant in a role-play setting. The interview must meet legal and corporate standards for conducting such interviews.

TASK: Developing marketing plans
Required Performance—Develop a marketing plan in response to realistic market and corporate conditions that meets the required corporate standards.

To What Standard?

School systems typically set standards at 70 percent to pass a course with a "C," 80 percent for a grade of "B," and 90 percent for an "A." Some set tougher standards. Most wind up curving or adjusting individual grades to fit the class' performance. There are no guarantees attached to school grades. A high grade does not mean that you can perform in the real world. It just means that you did well within the academic system. Many of humanity's great geniuses had lousy grades in school and then went on to make extraordinary contributions to society, and it's probably safe to say that many future geniuses will not fit the academic mold either.

Why do schools use normative grades that compare students to each other? Schooling is a long-term process stretched out over many years. Not everyone can qualify for all levels of schooling. School grades are part of an extensive selection system set up to weed the *academically* less talented out of the higher levels of schooling.

A business training program, however, is not spread out over years. It occurs in hours, days, or weeks. How well will each employee have to be able to perform the required tasks and skills in order to succeed in the program? A business training program is supposed to prepare all employees to do a job. You want the graduates of your training programs to have all the connections necessary to generate the appropriate job performances. If the employees can actually perform all the tasks and skills in realistic contexts, you can feel assured they will also be able to do the job to the same standards. That is why *good business training can guarantee its outcomes*.

How about pop quizzes, trick test items, and final exams? These practices are often part of academic programs. Why don't they have value in training programs as well? Business training is only concerned with those measurements that tell the instructor whether an employee's performance meets the standard. If the employee's performance does not meet the standard, you need coaching, counseling, and more relevant practice until it does. Good business training does not brand employees with C's or B's. Instead, it certifies graduates as competent to perform a job—no more and no less.

How should the instruction build the connections for performing each task or skill in each employee's brain? It leads employees through the necessary behavior until they can perform to the standard without assistance. Evaluation of employee learning consists of observing the employee performing the task or skill to standard. The employee must demonstrate his or her ability to perform a given task or skill before moving on to the next skill. The employee does this on his or her schedule, and evaluation takes place when the employee says so, not when the instructor says so. There is no point in evaluating the employee's performance if the employee judges that he or she still needs more practice. When the employee does demonstrate job competence, he or she can then move on to learn the next skill. The demonstration of competence ensures that the right connections have been made in the employee's brain to produce performance that meets the standard. It's a quality assurance measurement, and that's all it is. But that's a lot.

Does your company build anything without a quality assurance measurement? Not and stay competitive in today's markets. You do not count a product as being ready to move on to the next step in the manufacturing process or on to the distributor and to the end customer until it meets the standard for each step in the process. That's what total quality management and criterion-referenced instruction are all about.

Timing Your Training

The skills learned in a training program cannot be warehoused for use at some later time. Training must always be delivered "just in time." Why? Connections that aren't reinforced with use will not be maintained. Remember that inert knowledge is of no use to a business. It is a "use it or lose it" proposition. So do not train employees in new skills this year that they will not use until next year. If advance training is necessary, provide refresher training just before employees have to start using the new skills. The refresher training will take much less time to conduct than the original training, but it's absolutely necessary to ensure that performers are competent on the job from the beginning.

PROBE QUESTIONS

To recap, here are questions to ensure that employees practice each skill to competence.

For To-Be-Developed and Existing Training Programs

1. How will employees demonstrate their readiness to move on to the next unit of instruction?

   Reject or be skeptical about these kinds of responses:

   - The pace will be challenging. We are going to give some tough tests, just like what we use in our advanced university program. We'll assign grades and then we will move on.

2. Will all employees in a class move from one unit of instruction to the next as a group?

   Support or inquire into these kinds of responses:

   - Yes, but we will make arrangements for everyone to get all the practice he or she needs. The schedule is designed to allow this for virtually all employees who might take the program.

We have some skill enhancement practice available for those who finish a section very early.

Reject or be skeptical about these kinds of responses:

- Yes. There is a set schedule for this class, and we have to cover everything in a short period of time.

3. How will individual employees be assured of getting all the practice they need to master each skill? Is there assurance of there being enough practice exercises for all employees? Will this assurance be established in tryouts?

Support or inquire into these kinds of responses:

- We are building a file of real situations that have occurred on the job. If we run out of practice situations, we will be able to build new ones that are relevant very quickly from the file.

Reject or be skeptical about these kinds of responses:

- Practice will be in small groups. If an employee doesn't actually practice a problem, he or she will get to see or help someone else do it.

4. How will each employee establish his or her job competence of each skill? How will employee performance be judged and against what standards?

Support or inquire into these kinds of responses:

- We will have each technician demonstrate the skill while the instructor observes each one.

Reject or be skeptical about these kinds of responses:

- The instructor will walk around while the employees practice in small groups, making sure everyone gets a chance to practice. If the instructor has doubts about an employee's skill, he or she can suggest more practice.

Chapter 8

DOES PRACTICE EQUAL AT LEAST HALF OF TRAINING? Is the program efficient? Will each employee spend at least half of his or her time practicing needed skills?

Your Progress to This Point

- You have identified and documented a justifiable business need.

- You have established that the program will focus specifically on the skills employees need to learn.

- You have ensured that employees will be provided with relevant practice in realistic job formats.

- You have ensured that every employee will *practice* every skill to job competence and in a representative range of job situations.

Now you need to make sure the training program will be efficient.

What Is Training "Efficiency"?

Maximum training efficiency is the application of the least resources required to achieve the performance objectives. You improve efficiency by reducing the requirements for your most valued resources.

What is your most valued resource? Typically, the most valued resource in a corporation is its employees' time. Consequently, you set out to minimize the amount of time your employees must spend in training to achieve every performance objective required of them.

How do employees in a program spend their time? Let's examine the learning unit. What do employees do in working through a single module or learning unit? There are two major activities. First, employees get ready to practice and, second, they practice. Employees may do several things to get ready to practice:

- Read material telling them what they will have to do to demonstrate successful mastery of the skill.

- Watch a video explaining the relevance of the skill to the job.

- Watch a demonstration of the skill.

- Read about the safety practices and procedures for doing the skill.

- Read about how any equipment works and how to care for any tools used in performing the skill.

Whatever employees do to get ready to practice should take less time than they spend actually practicing the skill addressed by the module. The basic rule of thumb is that employees should spend *at least half* of their time in each unit actually practicing the skill addressed by the module.

Practice time includes time spent receiving feedback on each practice trial and guidance for improving performance on the next trial. If two employees practice together so that each provides feedback and guidance to the other, then only one employee's practice time should be used in comparing practice time to preparation time.

If you find that employees are achieving the performance objective but spending less time practicing than they spend in preparation, then you need to find some way to reduce the amount of prep time. Most often, you will find that the instructional unit is overburdened with unnecessary content. Fixing it is largely a matter of identifying the content that is actually needed to prepare the employee and deleting the rest.

Improving Practice Efficiency

Sometimes you can make practice itself more efficient by changing some of the practice conditions. Suppose you are training experienced technicians to disassemble and assemble a new model of a machine. They are already familiar with the old model and already know the functions of most of the components and how they fit together. You can structure most practice as dry runs (tell-and-point-to-without-actually-doing). You may be able to conduct three or four dry runs in the same amount of time it takes to do one full run. In this way, you can conduct the same number of practice trials in much less practice time. The last practice trial (or last few), however, should still be a full run.

Let's look at another common opportunity to make practice more efficient. Maybe you can provide faster feedback on each practice trial by switching from paper and pencil problems in which two employees help each other practice to computer-based instruction in which each employee practices alone. If you find such an opportunity, be sure that the value of the saved training time is worth more than the cost of developing the computer-based training materials. It's also important to be careful on this specific time-saving method. Feedback that comes without the employee's say-so (without the employee having time to think about an answer before opting to receive feedback) can actually disrupt the employee's understanding of what he or she has just done. Employees should have control over when they receive feedback in order to have the opportunity to reflect on their performance.

All of the benefits of a program change may not be limited to the classroom. For example, some format changes might have value in reducing future revision costs. In this case, some benefits show up in maintenance costs as well as delivery costs.

In some cases, changing the delivery medium can reduce delivery costs. Training originally designed to be delivered in two days in each of the company's regions would require employees to leave their jobs and go to a hotel in a nearby city where the program was delivered. If you change the program to computer-based training at each employee's workstation, employees work through the program as time is available on the job. For such a change to be worthwhile, housing, travel, and work-time savings over the remaining life of the program have to exceed the cost of developing and delivering the computer-based version.

Anytime you set out to improve the efficiency of a program, the value of the benefits obtained from the improvement should be greater than the cost of the improvement. You also have to ensure that the performance and conditions of practice in any alternative program are the same as that provided by the previous program. If they are, then the cost figures speak for themselves; if no, all bets are off. The alternative program may not be an effective replacement, regardless of how much it appears to save.

Suppose you had been training sales associates to deal with difficult customers by having them practice the skills in realistic role-play situations. Switching to a computer-based program in which they practice selecting from various strategies for dealing with various kinds of difficult customers is not as effective as actually handling a difficult customer. "Selecting how" is not the same as "doing." Or suppose you are training project managers to develop project plans by having them develop a plan for one of their own projects, which is then reviewed by an instructor who is also an expert project planner. Switching to a computer-based program with multiple-choice questions about the planning process and pre-set computer feedback is not nearly as effective as developing a plan. In fact, it may not work at all.

It is not the computer itself that invalidates these example practice situations, but rather changing the nature of the practice from that found on the job. We could have imposed the same kinds of invalid changes on classroom, instructor-led training. Computer-based programs, however, frequently *force* us to adopt invalid practice if we wish to conduct all instructional activities on the computer. Computer-based programs *can* often be used to prepare employees for practice by providing them with interactive animated graphics not available in any other medium. Typically, a mix of media is most effective for most training programs.

PROBE QUESTIONS

To recap, here are questions to ensure that your training programs are efficient.

For To-Be-Developed Training Programs

1. How will the developers protect against unnecessary content creeping into the program as it is being developed?

    Support or inquire into these kinds of responses:

    *   We will track every skill in the program to one or more tasks. The learning of "content" will be determined solely by the employee's application of that content in performing a skill. (*If they identify skills specifically and limit content to each single skill rather than to groups of skills, they should be able to avoid unnecessary content.*)

Reject or be skeptical about these kinds of responses:

- We have had top regional sales managers in the corporation go through texts and journal articles and select those that they judge to be most valuable for our sales staff and sales managers. Only the most valuable will be used.

For Existing Training Programs

1. Does experience with the program establish that each individual employee spends at least half of his or her time practicing the skills addressed by each unit of instruction?

Support or inquire into these kinds of responses:

- Yes, if you don't include the time they spend helping each other practice. In those cases each spends at least a third of his or her time practicing and another third or more helping others to practice.

Reject or be skeptical about these kinds of responses:

- Every employee spends at least half of his or her time practicing alone or as part of a group. When they practice in groups, each one performs a piece of the task, but they watch others in the group do other pieces.

Chapter 9

STEP 8 **WILL PRACTICES CAUSE NEGATIVE FEELINGS?** Are the instructional practices likely to produce anxiety, embarrassment, or frustration?

Your Progress to This Point

- You have identified and documented a justifiable business need.

- You have established that the program will focus specifically on the skills employees need to learn.

- You have ensured that employees will receive relevant practice in realistic job formats.

- You have ensured that every employee will practice every skill to job competence and in a representative range of job situations.

- You have made sure that employees will spend at least half of their time in training actually practicing.

Now you need to make sure that your employees will value the program and its outcomes. Why is that important? Let's consider the alternative.

Emotions and Learning

Are employees' feelings about the training they get important? Very much so. Feelings and emotions are not wispy things that afflict only the weak. There is real physiology and neurology underlying them. The sensations we experience as emotions and feelings are a result of muscular and glandular responses that prepare the body for action—fight, flight, or freeze. They are survival responses that have evolved over eons of animal existence. Without them, our ancestors would never have survived to produce us.

If a series of actions leads to an emotional response, then that response becomes part of the series of actions. However, it differs in that it is triggered early in the sequence, perhaps even by the initiating conditions in the situation (Damasio 1994).

Suppose you're painfully hurt falling off a ladder. The next time you climb a ladder, you may think, "This wound up being very painful before. Maybe I shouldn't do this or maybe I should proceed more carefully." Furthermore, the sensations generated by your emotional response trigger emotional patterns of thought and action that you learned in earlier experiences. You may think, "If I waiver, others will make fun of me. I'll bluster on even though I feel shaky and weak-kneed." That could be a dangerous way to proceed. The risk of making a critical mistake could be high in such a condition.

What are the likely effects on the learning process itself if employees experience strong negative emotions during training? The visceral sensations that result from negative emotional responses can be powerful. They can overwhelm all other inputs to the brain and initiate a train of thoughts and actions that are incompatible with learning. The employee can become disruptive or lose himself in a chain of ruminative thinking. Both interfere with learning.

Can negative emotions experienced during training affect later job performance? Indeed they can. Here are some likely possibilities.

- A supervisor in a program on how to deal with performance problems among subordinates is required to practice in role-playing exercises in front of the class. Many of the others in the class are more experienced supervisors. After each practice trial, the instructor encourages the class to criticize the employee's performance mercilessly. The instructor feels that it will help the employee to build confidence by "testing his wings" in tough situations. Do you think that the newly trained supervisor will try out his new skills on the job? Not likely.

- A technician in a class on how to operate a new piece of equipment goes through a number of stressful experiences. The instructor calls on her to answer complex theoretical questions orally before the whole class. If she hesitates, the instructor denigrates the technician for her slowness. If there is a mistake in her answer, the instructor tells the technician that her error has just blown up the whole plant and killed several operators. Then the class laughs at her. Is this technician likely to feel confident in her new skills when she returns to the job? Will she try to avoid working on the new equipment or call the help line to have an expert talk her through every little procedure?

Most of us witnessed or experienced these kinds of practices at some point in school. Do you remember the embarrassment or anger that the student on the receiving end felt at the time?

Traditional school tests are one of the principal sources of anxiety in our society. We may have nightmares about past school tests when we're going through anxious or stressful times later in life. Why?

- We are never sure what will be asked of us on the test and, hence, can never be certain that we are prepared.

- Major life paths are often opened or closed to us based on our performance on tests.

- There is usually no second chance.

- We must take the test when the instructor schedules it rather than when we are ready.

It's no wonder many students cheat and hate school—even some excellent scholars. I have met many workers who were undereducated because of these kinds of experiences in school. Ten or twenty years later, they are highly competent and skilled employees who are greatly valued by their employer. Still, even after years of success in their jobs, they flee from anything that even smacks of classroom instruction.

Preferred Motivational Conditions: Removing Unnecessary Stress

CRI by its very nature removes or avoids many of these all too common sources of anxiety and stress from the instructional situation. In criterion-referenced instruction, employees say when they are ready for the test at the end of each module of instruction. They know exactly what will be on the test because it is described in the objective given to them at the beginning and because it is exactly what they have been practicing. If they don't meet the standard the first time, an instructor coaches them and they practice until they feel that they are ready for the test again. If one employee needs more practice time than another employee, the employee gets it without recrimination. The instructor's role is to coach, advise, and encourage. Personal recriminations and put-downs are not practiced at all. Instructors engage in more quality coaching with employees who have difficulty learning the needed skills than they do with those who are able to cruise through the program. Instructors put their efforts where they are most needed.

One of the principal concerns of good CRI-based training is to build the employees' self-efficacy in their newly acquired skills (Bandura 1986). Given strong self-efficacy, they are willing and even eager to use those skills immediately upon returning to their jobs.

PROBE QUESTIONS

To recap, here are questions to ensure that employees will value the program and its outcomes.

For To-Be-Developed and Existing Training Programs

1. Is there any point in the program where employees will be required to recite or practice in front of other employees who are not involved in the mechanics of the practice situation itself? Can it be avoided?

Support or inquire into these kinds of responses:

- Role-playing exercises in a sales training program are done in rooms with just those employees who are participating.

Reject or be skeptical about these kinds of responses:

- Each team does role-plays in front of the class and receives feedback.

2. Will instructors be selected and/or trained to provide constructive feedback and guidance that focuses on the employee's performance without demeaning or belittling the employee?

Support or inquire into these kinds of responses:

- Instructors for the program are competent volunteers who have been judged by their supervisors and colleagues to have good people skills. They will also receive training on coaching.

Reject or be skeptical about these kinds of responses:

- We have selected the top performers in the job as instructors. Their feedback will be invaluable.

3. Will employees be required to take tests or skill checks at set times, regardless of whether they are ready?

Support or inquire into these kinds of responses:

- Everyone will be administered the performance tests at the same time, but not until each and every one has completed three successful practice trials.

Reject or be skeptical about these kinds of responses:

- Everyone will be tested at the same time on a set schedule. That will ensure that tests are fair.

4. Will employees' performance on skill checks be assigned differential grades and could other employees know these grades?

Support or inquire into these kinds of responses:

- All employees who finish the program will be designated as competent to do the job—nothing else.

Reject or be skeptical about these kinds of responses:

- Each employee's performance on skill checks will be posted on the bulletin board with errors marked and a grade. This will provide other employees with guidance and challenge.

5. Will competitive prizes be offered to employees for performance or speed in the program?

    Reject or be skeptical of competitive contests.

    *   There are always more losers than winners, and losing is not a pleasant emotional experience. Every employee who completes the program should be recognized as competent to perform the job.

Chapter 10

STEP 9 IS THE PROGRAM OF VALUE?

Your Progress to This Point

■ Congratulations, you have carried the decision process through to the end. You have a proposal for developing or customizing a criterion-referenced instruction program before you. It supports a critical corporate strategy. There's only one problem: the proposal includes a cost section that has left you with a paralyzing case of sticker shock. However, you have come this far, and you need to sort it out.

Putting Your Decision in Perspective

It can be difficult to understand the factors involved in a single choice because it lacks the perspective that comes with comparing several options. So let's put this decision in perspective by exploring other options. Let's assume that at this point in the process two of your assistants bring you other proposals from organizations in which they have strong contacts and in which they have a great deal of confidence.

- One is for a popular off-the-shelf program from a well-known, prestigious firm. A professional team of skilled and charismatic presenters will deliver the training. It includes several generic group practices that lead to insights into the processes addressed by the program. There are no evaluations of individual employee learning. The cost for this program is about half the cost of developing the CRI-based program.

- The other proposal is from a business school at one of the nation's leading universities. The university promises to deliver a straight subject matter program delivered by a team of professors and headed by one of the best-known authorities in the field. This team will administer traditional tests including multiple-choice, short answer, and essay questions. The course is organized around a complex case study that builds from one class to the next. Surprisingly, the cost of this program falls between the cost of the other two programs. Established thinkers in a field do not come cheap.

Which will you choose? More importantly, how will you go about making your choice?

The Cost of Developing and Delivering Training

To begin, don't be fooled into thinking you have the full cost of each of the proposed programs. All you have at this time is the vendor's proposed price for his product and services. This is the "sticker price." There are additional costs.

Hidden Design and Development Costs

The development of the CRI-based program requires that the vendor have access to expert performers in the company to gather information about the tasks, skills, work conditions and situations, and the employees to be trained. You may have to dedicate several performers to this activity for several weeks or months. There are direct costs for the performers' salaries and benefits for this period, and there may also be some indirect costs for the loss of productivity. In the case of the off-the-shelf program, design and development may already be mostly done and the costs amortized over the life of the program. This makes the program appear less expensive.

Delivery Costs

All of the proposed programs will need to be delivered, meaning there will likely be additional delivery costs not considered in the original cost proposals.

In the CRI-based program, it may be necessary to train individuals to deliver the instruction. For any of the three, if the training is going to be delivered in several different regions, there may be travel and housing costs for the trainers. In addition, employees may need to travel to a different city for the training, in which case there will be travel and housing costs for them. Employees will be absent from work while they are being trained. You need to include their salary and benefits costs and loss of productivity costs during the time they are in training.

Design, development, and delivery costs will not be the same for the three programs you are considering. You need to add the delivery cost to the sticker price to obtain the total cost for each program. The CRI-based program may be the most expensive to deliver because it requires every employee to practice every skill to job competence and because there are generally more instructors. The off-the-shelf program uses group practice and has no assessment of individual learning. Consequently, it requires fewer instructors and possibly less time. It is difficult to make a generalization about which program requires the most time, since the CRI-based program eliminates irrelevant content, thereby cutting down on delivery time. The subject matter program's lectures will be delivered by satellite television to all target employees at the same time. Multiple-choice tests on each lecture will be administered to each group before the next lecture, and employees receive grades on each test and on the final exam. The subject matter program takes employees off the job for the least amount of time.

Cost Versus Value

If you were only considering training costs in selecting a program, your decision would be fairly easy. Yet if you only consider costs, you will be misled most of the time. You need to consider the value of each program, rather than just its costs. To calculate value, you must determine how the benefits of the program outweigh its costs.

Value = Benefits – Costs

So far, you have only considered costs. Now you have to estimate the benefits most likely to accrue from each program. How do you do that?

What constitutes benefits for these programs? You want a program that develops employees who can do what they need to do on the job to help the company's business strategy to succeed as quickly as possible. This is exactly what CRI-based training is designed to do.

- It identifies what employees need to do to be successful in performing their jobs.

- It identifies what skills (including mental skills) employees need to learn in order to successfully perform their jobs.

- It leads them through doing those things they need to learn to do to succeed on the job.

- It determines competency by having each employee demonstrate that he or she can perform each skill before graduating from the training.

- It provides each employee with enough experience to ensure the employee's self-confidence and willingness to perform as desired.

The outcome is employees who return to their jobs and perform successfully immediately after training. What is completely successful training worth? Successful training resolves the problem that instigated the training and banishes the costs accruing from that problem. It is quite common for criterion-referenced programs to recoup the full costs of designing, developing, and delivering the programs many times over within the first year following their application to all the target employees. Why? Because CRI instills the necessary skills to ensure job success before employees leave training. There are no skills left to be learned later on the job.

What about the off-the-shelf generic performance program? What benefits accrue from it? This kind of program approximates what employees will need. It may even lead them to figure out what it is they need to do once they get on the job if the opportunity and encouragement exist. Some employees may not do too badly with this type of training: half of them may figure out how to do half the skills they need in their own job environments within six months. It may take them even longer to put all these skills together into effective job performances. Of the other half, a quarter may figure out how to do a quarter of the skills and the remaining quarter may not figure out any of it at all. Under optimum conditions, this type of training will produce less than half the benefits that accrue to the criterion-referenced program. Often, it will be substantially less. Graduates of generic performance training programs typically exhibit a substantial learning curve on the job after training is over (though not nearly as substantial as that exhibited by graduates of traditional academic programs). Graduates of criterion-referenced programs typically exhibit no learning curve or only a very slight one.

What about the academic program? Those who complete this program may figure out how to apply some of what they've learned on the job, but it will take quite a while. There will be no instructor present after training to provide guidance and feedback. Employees may try something and then have to wait to see how it works. That is a slow and uncertain way to learn. Only those who are highly motivated and who encounter supportive conditions on the job are likely to try to apply the concepts in their work. They will also need to be sufficiently intelligent to translate abstract concepts into concrete applications. Some may try a few things, but for the most part they will be confused as to what to do and demoralized by failures during training and on the job. The results of this kind of program are more likely to be negative. The costs of the program, although not as high as the costs of the criterion-referenced program, simply make the consequences more dire.

Costs are often poor indicators of value. When you evaluate the relative merits of various training options, base your evaluation on value to the corporation rather than simply on cost. Ask yourself what the consequences will be for the business if these skills are not provided to the targeted employees. What will happen to the company's product? How much rework will be needed? What happens to sales and market share? Estimate a conservative dollar value for these effects, being sure to include cascading effects.

Conversely, if these skills *are* provided to the targeted employees and used effectively by them on the job, what will be the positive results for the business? In this case, you are more likely to encounter alternative possibilities. Positive outcomes are often more difficult to predict than negative outcomes. Identify the more significant possibilities and value them separately. You can assign probabilities to the various possibilities as a way of firming up your choices. Estimate a conservative dollar value for these effects. Focus on quantifiable benefits.

Now you can see what the benefits or consequences will be if you do or do not implement an effective program. You may need the help of a qualified performance technologist to help you determine the benefits that are most likely to accrue from your training options. Again, you may find the expertise you need right in your own training department.

Developing Creative Options

You do not necessarily have to restrict your decision to just choosing among the options. In our example, for instance, you might decide to try a melding of the three options. You might decide that the university professor is an outstanding asset as a consultant, even though you do not care for his training approach since it does not offer the best value for your training dollar. You might also decide that the off-the-shelf program contains some proprietary content of considerable merit. Consequently, you decide to build a criterion-referenced program around the off-the-shelf program. The off-the-shelf program will have to be customized to suit your corporation's activities and situations. You further decide that the source for the customization should be the vendor (or internal training function) that proposed developing the criterion-referenced program. That vendor is the most likely to possess the high level of performance technology and skill needed to make the customization work most effectively. Can you bring these three sources of separate expertise together to develop the strongest possible program at a cost that produces sufficient value for your corporation? Try it. Be creative in forming the best tools for your corporation, its owners, and its employees.

In the next couple of chapters, we move on to talk about the realities and the technicalities of trying to make smart decisions about training in any organization. The next chapter takes you through using *The Path to Smart Training Decisions* flowchart and worksheet to develop a training proposal and to determine value. Finally, there are some tips on communicating with various groups within and outside your corporation—groups whose support can be instrumental in implementing an effective training program.

Chapter 11

Determining the Value of Individual Training Programs

You will find the *Path to Smart Training Decisions* flowchart and worksheet most useful (1) to select the best of two or more proposals for meeting the same training requirement, and (2) to document and defend your selection to other levels of management. Training proposals can differ in many ways, but with *The Path to Smart Training Decisions* you can arrive at a single value for each proposal as a basis for comparing it to others.

Many of your training decisions will either be focused on shaping and valuing one of your own training proposals to persuade an internal client or evaluating the merits of someone else's proposal. But when you have programs for different groups of employees who require training in different skills, determining the value of proposed training programs can become much more complicated.

Whenever you are considering several training programs to support a single business strategy, you must distribute the resources available for training and the impact of each training program among the several programs that are needed. The entire budget is not available for just one training program, and the entire impact does not come from just one program. Use a separate worksheet for each training program, rather than trying to use just one.

When you are forced to consider a program that does not meet all of the requirements laid out in steps 1 through 9, the worksheet can be extremely helpful in making your case for you. Numbers may be able to speak volumes in a situation in which you cannot turn down a program flat out.

Another common complication is the problem of employees not being able to go directly to their jobs after training. Suppose your company is installing a new database to be used by customer reps, product managers, production managers, accounting personnel, shipping personnel, and so on. With a cutover date six months from now, you can't possibly pull everyone off their jobs at the same time and train all of them; you need to stay in business while training takes place. Instead, you train employees in batches. Consequently, some will be trained six months before cutover date, some four months before, two months before, and right before. The skills of those trained well before cutover will deteriorate if they are not used. How do you make sure that everyone's new skills are up to required job standards at cutover?

In this situation, you need to develop a supplementary program to augment skills that have gone stale through disuse. Typically, the solutions are to develop transitional job aids for immediately following cutover and to provide refresher practice right before cutover. This refresher practice program will be much shorter than the original training program. It will probably be short enough to run everyone through it just two or three days before cutover during a brief overtime period or two.

The following example walks you through a sample training proposal development, using the worksheet to evaluate the proposal. It is not meant to address all of these complications, only to give you an idea of how *The Path to Smart Training Decisions* flowchart and worksheet can work to your advantage.

Here's the Situation You Face

You are the training manager in a major financial products and services company. The company depends on its call center sales force to generate about half of its revenue. It has three call centers in the United States and two in Asia and South America.

You were recently part of the guidance committee in a study to determine the effectiveness of your call center sales associates. An outside consulting firm conducted the study. The research team recorded and analyzed a large random sample of telephone transactions over a six-month period. In about half those calls, sales associates failed to identify the customers' needs and, consequently, did not propose appropriate products and services to the customers. As a result, a large number of customers did not renew the products and services they had been receiving and went to a competitor. Other customers were grossly undersold or sold products and services they did not need. The lost revenue was estimated at $150 million annually. The company's current annual revenue from its call centers is about $500 million.

Currently, senior sales associates at each call center train new sales associates. None of them like to do it because training a new hire cuts into their time and commissions. Each senior sales associate does whatever he wants to do when training a new sales associate. Attempts to formalize the training program in the past have not met with great success.

The VP in charge of the call centers asks you to develop or purchase a training program to remedy these problems. She wants every sales associate re-trained within the next six months, and she doesn't want sales associates pulled off their jobs any more than absolutely necessary. She would prefer to deliver the training at the associates' own work stations with a two-hour global satellite hook-up to kick it off. You ask for several days to investigate the problem and develop a proposal. She agrees.

Your Investigation and the Results

You assign both of your performance analysts to develop target population descriptions of the sales associates and to conduct the training analysis.

The target populations. Your performance technologists found two clearly different target populations.

1. The sales associates in the United States are mostly female (90 percent). All are high school grads; many have some college, and about 30 percent are college grads. Their ages range from twenty to sixty, with the median about thirty-five. Most view the sales associate position as temporary until something better turns up. About 15 percent have been with the company at least ten years. Turnover in the position runs 40 to 50 percent per year. It is an entry-level position with very little opportunity for advancement or transfers to other departments. There are approximately 150 sales associates in this group.

2. The sales associates in other countries are 50 percent male and 50 percent female. They are all college graduates. Their ages range from twenty-four to thirty-two with the average about twenty-seven. They view their jobs as long-term since few jobs in their countries

pay as well. There is virtually no turnover in the position. They all speak English fluently, but are not fluent in American idioms. These sales associates conduct their calls in English to customers in Canada and Europe. There are approximately 100 sales associates in these groups.

The skill deficiencies. Virtually all the sales associates were very weak in many basic job skills. Those few US sales associates who had been on the job for five or more years were very skilled in all aspects of the job. Over the years, they had figured out how to do things and practiced until they were proficient.

Most of the sales associates in all locations were unable to conduct an effective inquiry into a client's financial needs. They did not ask questions about significant characteristics of the client's business portfolios and did not present their questions in a friendly and interested way. They were often abrupt or curt. They were not able to relate the company's products and services to the client's needs. For the most part, they simply resold products and services the customer was already receiving.

Your proposal. You decide to recommend training on two levels. The first level will provide instruction and practice for dealing with the most common kinds of client interactions. The second level will be delivered two months later and deal with less common and more difficult kinds of client interactions. Sales associates will be able to consolidate new basic skills on the job before learning more advanced skills.

Each level, in turn, will be divided into two phases. The first phase will be delivered through the company intranet at each sales associate's workstation. In this phase, each associate will practice developing appropriate questions to ask clients in realistic situations. You want them to practice forming questions in their own words rather than choosing from a list. Consequently, you propose that associates type their questions onto their screens in their own words. For feedback, they will compare their questions to a graded series of questions presented in a split window. They will also be given a list of key points to look for.

In the second phase, associates will practice delivering their questions in role-playing exercises. You propose setting up several rooms at each call center where three associates can go to practice together. Associates will be provided with unscripted role-plays that specify characteristics to be enacted by the associate playing the part of the client. One associate will serve as observer and recorder using a prepared checklist of key points. The three will debrief after each role play.

All training will be self-paced. Each associate must achieve the job standard on each skill before progressing to the next skill. You propose to divide the associates at each call center into five groups, with only one group being trained at a time. Completing the training in phases will lessen the impact on day-to-day operations. Furthermore, each group will spend only half of each workday in training, spending the rest of the time on the job. This will help them build their new skills into their job performance right away.

You also want to have a facilitator available at each site to coach employees and to encourage them to progress. You figure a part-time facilitator will be sufficient when employees are working at their own workstations, but you want a full-time facilitator available during the role-playing phase. You decide you can use a local lead sales associate for $30/hour at each site.

The three US centers have substantial turnover. Replacements will also need to be trained. Though there's a chance the training could affect that turnover rate, you still need to calculate the expected cost to train new hires if turnover remains the same. However, the training programs you are developing will be designed for sales associates who have experience on the floor rather than for new hires. You decide to keep the current informal training practices for new hires for their first month on the job. After that, they will have had sufficient experience on the floor to be able to enter the new training programs, but you need to add the cost of delivering the new training to them to your proposal budget. The expected turnover rate for the three US centers is 40 percent.

You propose setting up a guidance committee for the project, which includes the key stakeholders and your VP. You want to be sure you have her clout when you need it to get around roadblocks and through bottlenecks.

Since you know you don't have the staff to develop the needed training, you propose bringing in a training development contractor to do most of the work. You also propose assigning the most senior US sales associates to serve as job performance experts (JPE) for the training developers. You ask to have at least half of their time dedicated to that role during the training development. Your staff will serve as project monitors, coordinators, and problem solvers for the contract developers.

Cost. Lost revenue will be the biggest cost involved in the training. Sales associates (SAs) currently generate about $2.27 million per day. If the training takes ten half days on average, then lost revenue will be approximately $11.35 million. You propose overtime for the 80 percent of the sales associates not in training at any given time so that revenue will not be lost.

You and your staff make rough estimates of how long each training program will be on average. You decide on four half days for the first level (computer-based) and six half days for the role-playing phase for a total of ten half days. You come up with the following cost estimates for the project.

1.	Wages for SAs during training @ $20/hr	$200,000.00
2.	Overtime	$300,000.00
3.	Training development contract	$300,000.00
4.	JPE time (5 JPEs half time for three months plus lost revenue)	$680,000.00
5.	Facilitators	$26,400.00
6.	Training costs for turnover new hires in US over five-year period	$271,680.00
	Total for training	**$1,778,080.00**

You're certain this is more than the VP is expecting. To keep those costs in perspective, you add three lines to your budget.

Expected revenue increase at end of first year	$150,000,000
Expected profit increase at end of first year	$15,000,000
Expected benefit life of the training program	Five years

Your Presentation to the VP

The VP says exactly what you expect her to say. " For that kind of money, I can send a bunch of them to business school for their MBAs!" First, you point out the revenue increases that the program is expected to generate. This is a conservative expectation. The VP understands the possible gains, but doesn't understand why the training can't be completed in one or two days instead of ten half days. She feels that you should be able to tell the employees about the skills, let them practice once or twice in training, and then let them practice on the job. You reply that it would decrease costs, but it would also virtually wipe out expected revenue and profit increases. It *would* cost less but yield **no** gain.

Next, you give her a quick overview of the differences between the academic and business training paradigms (appendix A). Learning for application is not a matter of storing information in memory; rather it is a matter of practicing the applications. Business is concerned with immediate application: doing, not talking about. The employee's mistakes should happen during training where they can be corrected at no cost, not on the job where they can adversely impact the business.

With all of this information before her, the VP agrees to support the proposal, with the reminder that her neck is on the block as well. You thank her for her support and reassure her that the program will work. You also ask her to consider letting you develop an incentive program for the sales associates based on increases in revenue following the training. You explain that the sales associates themselves will resist taking time away from their jobs and commissions to go through training unless they see a larger payoff in the future for them. She agrees. The two of you agree to set aside 2 percent of the expected revenue gains for the incentive program—$3 million. The VP came up through sales, so she understands incentives even if she doesn't understand training—yet. You will need to include the incentives program as a second component in this business strategy when you're calculating value.

The Worksheet

Now let's review how you would fill out *The Path to Smart Training Decisions* worksheet as you were developing the proposal.

STEP 1. IS THERE A BUSINESS NEED?

Is there a substantial need for new training?

Yes. You made a few notes in this section regarding significant background issues and a thumbnail description of the two target populations.

Program Title: Sales Information and Planning

Source: VP of Sales

Describe the business need this program addresses: Improve the quality of sales telephone contacts. Outside study estimates that inadequate sales planning results in $150 million in lost revenue per annum. Customers are being undersold, sold improper products or services (possible legal risk), or lost as customers because of a failure to fit proposals to customer needs.

What position(s) will be trained? Call center sales associates

Number of employees to be trained: Approximately 250.

Gender: US reps are 90% female. Overseas reps are 50/50 male/female.

Locations(s) of employees: 150 in 3 US call centers, 50 each in 2 call centers in Asia and South America.

General level of education: US reps have some college or are college grads. All overseas reps are college grads.

Primary language(s): English

General turnover rate: High turnover (40%) in US call centers. There is virtually no turnover in the overseas call centers.

Other defining characteristics: US reps tend to view the sales associate position as a temporary position until something better turns up. Overseas reps are stable employees, view the sales associate position as long-term. Overseas reps conduct their calls in English to customers in Canada and Europe.

STEP 2. IS THE FOCUS ON PERFORMANCE?

Does the program focus on things you want trainees to _do_ that they aren't able to do now?

Yes.

Briefly identify the desired performance(s): Qualifying customer, asking customer questions based on info in system and customer responses to identify customer needs, selecting products and services that best fit customer's needs, presenting proposal, and closing, if appropriate.

STEP 3. ARE TASKS AND SKILLS DETAILED?

Have the specific job tasks and skills needed by the target employees been named and described in detail? If not, will they be?

Yes. The training developers will identify and analyze the tasks and skills required by the job, build skill hierarchies, and identify the skills that need training.

STEP 4. IS PRACTICE REALISTIC?

Will employees practice the job skills they need to learn in realistic job contexts?

Yes. You convinced the VP of the importance of relevant practice so that mistakes happen in training and not on the job. The contractors under the supervision of your performance analysts will design the practice situations.

STEP 5. DOES PRACTICE INCLUDE A MIX OF JOB SITUATIONS?

Is practice provided in a representative mix of job situations?

Yes. The audio tapes made by the outside consulting company when they audited the calls are available. They will be reviewed to develop representative situations.

STEP 6. DO LEARNERS PRACTICE TO JOB COMPETENCE?

Will each employee's job competence in each skill be verified during the program?

Yes. Each associate must achieve the job standard on each skill before progressing to the next skill.

Determining the Value of Individual Training Programs

STEP 7. DOES PRACTICE EQUAL AT LEAST HALF OF TRAINING?

Is the program efficient? Will each employee spend at least half his or her time practicing needed skills?

Yes. You expect associates to spend three-quarters of their time in training actually practicing. They will not practice skills unnecessarily because the training will be self-paced. As soon as an associate demonstrates competence on a skill, he or she moves on to the next skill.

STEP 8. WILL PRACTICES CAUSE NEGATIVE FEELINGS?

Are the instructional practices likely to produce anxiety, embarrassment, or frustration?

No. Role-playing exercises will take place with only the associates involved in the exercise present. There will not be any public role-plays in front of the entire class. Associates will not be asked to practice skills they are not prepared for or to demonstrate competence before they feel ready. Consequently, failure experiences will be minimized. Nor will associates be held back because others in the class have not progressed as rapidly. Instructors will be selected and trained to provide constructive, positive coaching.

STEP 9. IS THE PROGRAM OF VALUE?

1. **What are the expected financial gains from the success of the business strategy that the program addresses (profits per year)?**

   It would be misleading to estimate the benefits of the business strategy as the expected revenue increase. It is more reasonable to use the profits yielded by the revenue increase. The company generally experiences a 10 percent profit from revenues, so you enter "$15 million."

2. **Conservatively estimate what percentage of the expected gains from the business strategy can be credited to the success of just this training program.**

   Isolating the effects of a training program is itself a very complicated issue. *Return on Investment in Training and Performance Improvement Products* (2000) by Jack J. Phillips is an excellent reference on this topic. For the purpose of this example, we'll say that 50 percent of the gains can be credited to the training program and 50 percent to the incentives program.

3. **Multiply line 1 and line 2. This is the annual benefit which can be attributed to the strategy.**

    $15 million multiplied by .5 is $7.5 million.

4. **What is the expected benefit life of the program (in years)?**

    Five years is the expected benefit life.

5. **Multiply line 3 and line 4. This is the optimal benefit attributable to the training over the life of the program.**

    This gives you a total estimated benefit of $37.5 million.

6a. **What proportion of the program's skills will graduates be able to perform to standard at graduation?**

    Since the learning standard is job competence and since an associate cannot progress from one skill to the next until she achieves that standard on her present skill, clearly the associate will have demonstrated the ability to perform all skills to standard at graduation. Hence, the proportion is 1.00.

6b. **What proportion of the program's skills will graduates be able to perform to standard six months after graduation?**

    Associates will return to their jobs immediately after training. There will be no loss in their newly acquired skills from disuse. They will apply them every day on the job. Hence, the proportion again is 1.00.

    (Note: If you were dealing with a training program in which you were training employees in shifts leading up to one cutover date, you would need to consider that here. If, like the example at the beginning of the chapter, many of your employees have been away from training for a while, you would need to consider supplementary training such as transitional job aids and refresher practice. Don't forget to include the development and implementation costs for these items in the cost of the overall program.)

6c. **Average these two proportions. This is the expected effectiveness of the training program.**

    The average of 1.00 and 1.00 is 1.00. Hence, the expected effectiveness of the training program is 1.00.

7. **Multiply line 5 and line 6c. This is the expected net benefit of the training program.**

   $37.5 million times 1.00 equals $37.5 million in expected benefit over five years.

8. **How much will the program cost to acquire and to maintain over the life of the program?**

   You calculated this figure in your proposal. The total was $1,778,080.

9. **Subtract line 8 (cost) from line 7 (net training benefits). This number represents the value of the training program.**

   Line 8 ($37.5 million) minus line 7 ($1,778,080) equals a value of $35,721,920.

10. **Calculate the benefit/cost ratio by dividing line 7 by line 8.**

    Line 7 divided by line 8 gives you a benefit/cost ratio of 21:1.

While this example doesn't reflect all of the complications one could come across when developing a training proposal, hopefully it's given you a better idea of the things you might encounter in a real training situation. What's likely, however, is that people in your organization who are unfamiliar with CRI—people whose support you will usually need—will have misconceptions and concerns. The next chapter addresses some of the most likely ones and gives some tips for dealing with them.

Chapter 12

Communicating Inside and Outside the Corporation

No training department works alone, and there are a number of groups whose support can make or break a worthwhile training program proposal. Several corporate populations—both inside and outside the company—need information on the technology of CRI:

- Upper-level managers and executives;

- Non-training managers;

- Employees who will participate in CRI-based programs;

- Corporate trainers and training developers not trained in the technology for developing and delivering CRI programs;

- Training vendors and consultants who sell training programs to the corporation or develop them for the corporation.

It's important to remember that each of these populations needs somewhat different information because each has different concerns about training. In this chapter, we review some of the different concerns you might encounter and suggest ways of dealing with them, whether distributing reading materials or conducting presentations. And remember, a "presentation" could range from a spur of the moment discussion with the division vice president to a formal presentation to a group of managers or employees.

Appendices A, B, and C can help you in making persuasive and substantive presentations. You can use these tools to guide your discussions with other people on important instructional issues.

- **Appendix A:** *Instructional Paradigms: Academic vs. Business.* How the business and academic instructional paradigms differ and why.

- **Appendix B:** *How People Really Learn (With Implications for Training).* Why criterion-referenced instruction works so well.

- **Appendix C:** *Criterion-Referenced Instruction for Today's Business Needs.* Short benefits-oriented piece for upper-level executives.

These pieces are based on twenty-five years' worth of experience in CRI with clients throughout the world. In my experience, the instructional paradigm presentation is particularly powerful and effective. Talking points are included to remind you of some of the issues you can raise during these discussions and ways to rebut misconceptions that are raised by others. Some other tips: don't try to say everything that is provided for any single chart, and pick your points to fit the individual or small group to whom you are talking.

When you are ready to seek support from a specific group, decide which points are relevant. Review the concerns listed for each relevant population; these concerns also provide guidance regarding which charts or articles to use for your presentation. Then review the discussion points for your selected charts.

It's also a good idea to be prepared to back up your decision process. Why should others trust that the program you're recommending is the best? Why is it the best? Understanding how a decision was made can help to build trust and support. Use *The Path to Smart Training Decisions* to explain the most important components of a training program. Once you've gone through the differences between the instructional paradigms (appendix A), the decision process will make more sense.

Upper-Level Managers and Executives

Concerns
Upper-level managers and executives are concerned with developing strategies to deal with changing business, technological, or market conditions. Many of

the business strategies they consider will require that existing employees perform in different ways than they have in the past.

If upper-level managers and executives have little or no knowledge of CRI, they may well make ineffective plans for implementing business strategies. That happens all the time with disappointing to disastrous consequences. "Criterion-Referenced Instruction for Today's Business Needs" (appendix C) can inform them of the kind of instructional power available today. This brief and direct paper was written with this population of readers in mind and addresses the issues on which they need to be informed in order to make good decisions.

Sometimes, simply distributing this information can rally the support you need. However, it is more likely that you will need to follow up with additional information. The charts with their associated discussion points can help you plan and deliver face-to-face presentations.

Upper-level managers and executives may not always recognize the performance changes that will be needed to turn their business strategies into reality. You may have to lead them through identifying the necessary changes in job performance. Some of the changes may require that employees learn new skills, which means they will need training. If you have not learned enough about performance technology to do this, then find someone in your training department or a performance consultant to help you.

The level of trust that upper-level managers and executives have in business training is often determined by the beliefs they have about instruction. Make some casual inquiries to find out in advance what kinds of misconceptions you're likely to encounter. Here are some of the misconceptions you may find during your inquiries.

MISCONCEPTIONS

- Instructional programs are not effective, but they are important contributors to corporate image.

- Instructional programs are not effective, but labor expects or requires us to provide them.

- The amount that students learn in an instructional program depends largely on student intelligence and motivation.

- Good instructional programs always consist of quality presentations prepared and delivered by experts in the field.

- The evaluation of students and instructional programs must always be through traditional knowledge tests.

- Fair and accurate grades that differentiate among the students in the class must be used in instructional programs to identify the most promising students.

- Managers and professionals need to be "educated" rather than "trained." Training is appropriate for manual workers and shift workers, but not for generalists.

If you encounter many of these misconceptions, conduct discussions with them based on the following two charts and their associated discussion points:

✓ **Instructional Paradigms: Academic vs. Business**

✓ **How People Really Learn (With Implications for Training)**

Stress the fact that criterion-referenced instruction can guarantee performance. CRI will greatly increase the likelihood of success of the corporation's business strategies. The effectiveness of the training is as critical to the corporation as the success of the business strategies the training supports. It's important to remember that presentations to upper-level managers and executives need to be brief, to the point, and well organized.

Non-training Managers

Concerns

Non-training managers are principally concerned with achieving goals in the activities they manage. Those goals will often require that employees perform more effectively, more efficiently, more cooperatively, and with more innovation. Employees often will need to learn new technical and social skills, and managers and supervisors will need to learn new ways of managing employees.

Like upper-level executives, the trust that managers put in business training is influenced by the beliefs they have acquired about instruction. Make some casual inquiries to find out in advance what kinds of misconceptions are common or strongly held by the managers in your corporation. Here are some misconceptions you may find.

MISCONCEPTIONS

- Training is an intrusive activity that takes my people off the job, usually when I need them most.

- Training is a reward given to good performers so that they can rest and have fun for a while.

- Employees need training to get the right background information. They need experience on the job and coaching after training to become competent. The only way to learn to do a job is by doing it.

- Training has never helped my employees do the job. Its only purpose is to satisfy the union and regulatory agencies.

If you encounter many of these misconceptions, consider including information from the following chart and its associated talking points:

✓ Instructional Paradigms: Academic vs. Business

Stress the fact that in criterion-referenced instruction, employees practice the skills necessary for the job during training. Employees learn by doing, but not in a haphazard, drawn-out process. Rather, they learn through a carefully designed, highly efficient process that gets them up to speed as quickly as possible.

Stress that there are many ways CRI can be administered, meaning you can work with the manager to develop training that will intrude on regular operations as little as possible. It does not have to be classroom instruction that pulls a large number of workers off the line at the same time. In some instances, the function could operate its own training program using employees you've trained to manage programs designed by performance technologists. A great deal depends upon what kinds of skills the employees need to practice and the resources available.

You may need to have two or three meetings with activity managers. In the first meeting, just focus on selling the approach. In the following meetings, determine which training arrangements will best meet their needs with the least intrusion on the activity's operation. Start laying the groundwork for a long-term working partnership between the function and the training department.

Employees or Learners in CRI-Based Programs

Concerns

Employees want to have the skills they need to succeed in their jobs. Many of them may think they already have all the skills they need, and they may be right. Others may not have all the skills, but they think they do or they don't want to be exposed as not having those skills. Others know they don't have the skills and are eager to learn them.

The feelings that employees have about training are often determined by the experiences they have had in school and in previous business training programs. There is often the misconception that all schooling and training are the same. Employees may be wary of training because they believe the unpleasantness they experienced in past instructional events is about to happen to them again. Make some casual inquiries to find out in advance what kinds of feelings are common in the employees in your company. Here are some of the feelings you may find during your inquiries.

FEELINGS ABOUT TRAINING

- School/training didn't do much for me. I learned my job on the job. That's the only way to learn.

- I never did well in school. I always did poorly on tests and couldn't answer questions in class. It made me feel stupid.

- I always did well in school, so I know I'll shine in training. I can always cram at the last minute and do well.

- It's time to hide. I'll find a seat in the back row and slouch down so I won't be seen. There probably won't be any tests so I won't have to worry about being noticed.

- This is a waste of time. I don't need this.

If you encounter many of these attitudes, consider having a discussion with the employees based on the following chart:

✓ Instructional Paradigms: Academic vs. Business

Stress the differences between the academic and business paradigms in "Processes" and in "Evaluation." Also, stress that, wherever possible, practice is private. The training consists of practicing bits and pieces of the job and doing each piece over and over again until it is done right. Employees get all the practice they need to meet the job performance standards. They also get individual feedback and coaching. CRI-based programs are designed to make the employees feel comfortable and free of anxiety.

Corporate Trainers and Training Developers

Concerns

If you have decided to convert your training department from traditional training to CRI, you probably will need to win over the trainers and training developers. The trainers and training developers are experienced and skilled in developing and delivering traditional subject matter instruction or performance-enhanced subject matter instruction. Several of them may have been recognized within the company and by local professional organizations for their traditional classroom skills. Many of them have worked hard over the years to learn presentation skills. How do you win their support?

First, explain the differences between traditional and criterion-referenced instruction to them. For this, you can hold a series of discussions based on the following charts and their associated talking points:

✓ **Instructional Paradigms: Academic vs. Business**

✓ **How People Really Learn (With Implications for Training)**

Many trainers and training developers will see the merits of this approach based on this information. Some may not. During discussions, try to be attentive to fears and concerns raised either directly or indirectly. Here are some possible concerns you may encounter during these sessions and some ways of defusing them.

FEARS AND HOW TO DEFUSE THEM

> ■ *"You're telling us that everything we've done in the past is wrong. Yet our past work has been recognized by our peers and by management. We're not ready to change what worked for us in the past."*

> Stress that we live in a time when many old technologies are being replaced by new ones, and no field is immune to that. Their present skills will still be valued. The ability to communicate clearly, to explain difficult concepts, to coach employees, and to give useful feedback and guidance

will continue to be of significant value. They will use these skills in somewhat different situations, but the skills are the same.

■ *"Changing what we do this drastically will also change how we are valued by the corporation. Such a change endangers the positions of seniority and leadership for which we have worked so hard."*

Stress that the company will make sure they get the best training and on-the-job coaching to make the change successfully. *The company is committed to this change.* It will put management procedures in place to ensure that training programs in the future are developed and delivered in accordance with this new technology.

■ *"One major reason we are trainers is because we enjoy explaining concepts and procedures and enjoy dealing with and motivating groups of students."*

Trainers will still be interacting with employees. They will still be explaining difficult concepts and procedures and dealing with and motivating employees. However, now they will be doing these things with individuals in one-on-one situations. They will also be explaining difficult concepts and procedures through the design of effective instructional materials and presentations.

■ *"We understand your desire for results on the job. We think we can get them for you without doing this rigid analytical two-step dance. There are ways to increase transfer from the classroom to the job without losing the creativity and fun we give our students."*

Point out that participating employees will experience positive feelings during the program. You want to continue to emphasize concern with employee comfort and enjoyment in programs in the future. Discovery and experiential exercises can be useful in persuading employees to change how they perform. But persuasion has to be followed with practice to provide employees with the competence and self-efficacy to apply their new skills on the job. There is no need for fun and games to make training less onerous, because CRI-based training is not onerous to begin with.

Outside the Corporation: Dealing With Vendors and Consultants

Most corporations today rely on vendors and consultants for much of their training. Vendors develop off-the-shelf programs based on their apparent expertise in a topic or process. Typically, the vendor's primary claimed benefit to the customer is his or her expertise rather than the effectiveness of the instructional program. Even if claims of expertise are genuine, the instructional effectiveness of the program may be in doubt.

Vendors of expensive off-the-shelf programs often create a lot of excitement during the training in lieu of job competence as a training outcome. Why? Because they are as unsophisticated in assessing the value of training as the training market in general. You will want to use the *Path to Smart Training Decisions* worksheet to assess the potential value of any off-the-shelf programs you are considering for your company.

Some vendor programs are of good value. The best of these typically provide employees with generic situations as examples and early practice, but ask employees to use their own work contexts and situations for final practice and skill checks.

Customizing Vendor Programs

In many vendor programs, the vendors customize their basic programs for each customer. The vendor collects information about certain characteristics of the company, its personnel, the kinds of things it does, and the contexts in which it does them. This information is used to design highly realistic examples, practice problems, and skill checks for inclusion in their standard program.

Somewhat more commonly, you will find vendors who offer programs that provide *generic* examples and *generic* practice only. In some instances, the program is organized around a fixed and highly structured case study. Guiding a group through a case study as if they were performing it as a work team is not the same as providing individuals with practice in the skills needed to perform competently on a real team in a real situation. Group performance case study programs usually result in many employees not learning the skills well enough to perform competently or at all. Revising these programs to focus on individual skills rather than on the case study may be difficult. It may be easier to start program development from scratch.

Other vendor programs that use generic examples but are focused on skills are much easier to revise to obtain full value. Think of them as customizable programs. Use *The Path to Smart Training Decisions* flowchart and worksheet to help you identify what aspects need customization.

Motivational Programs That Don't Motivate for Long

You will find a number of vendor programs that don't even pretend to adhere to the business paradigm. They are often put on by exciting presenters who use glitzy multimedia techniques or prestigious professors with incredible reputations. They may present an informational program about new technology or a "motivational" program. In either case, have a performance technologist check these programs for hidden performances. Poor motivation can usually be traced to improper incentives in the workplace, changed conditions that require new skills, or inappropriate habits of thought that are self-defeating. "Pumping people up" is exciting at the moment, but it doesn't have a lasting effect. Finding the real source of the problem can lead to a solution that does have a lasting effect and usually costs less than having a motivational speaker come in to inspire employees—again and again.

When You Want the Expertise But Not the Package

How do you deal with vendors who have the expertise your company wants but who don't have it packaged in such a way as to yield full value to your company? First, acknowledge their expertise. Let them know that you value their expertise. And because you value it, you want to make sure your company obtains full value. You don't want to change or water down their expertise, but you want to repackage it to make it of even greater value. What are the fears and concerns they may have about your request?

Many vendors will not be open to the idea of changing their product. They may have the opinion that if you want what they sell, you have to take it the way it's packaged. This attitude can be difficult to deal with. Can you buy the vendor's materials and build your own training program around them? If you can, you are still paying the expert for information but you control how that information is delivered. You may even want to hire the vendor as a consultant. In this scenario, you would have to delay the training until your program is ready. There is no instant gratification this way, but delayed gratification is better than none at all.

If the vendor's expert information is not publicly available, then you'll need to ask yourself how much of the information belongs only to the vendor. It may be that the ideas are public, but the vendor has pulled them together, given them a name, and popularized them. If this is the case (and it usually will be), then you can have your developers or contractors develop a better program using the publicly available ideas for application in your company. Don't use the vendor's names, labels, or proprietary ideas. You won't have the vendor's prestige attached to your programs and that may be a sticking point with some of your company's managers and executives. If you can get the money, consider doing both: bring in the vendor's program and design your program as a supplement to it.

In Conclusion: Today's Challenge and the Great Promise It Holds

The greatest challenge facing training and performance professionals today is educating internal customers and executives to use the full power of today's performance and training technologies. Management processes and practices have dramatically improved over the last two decades, but training, for the most part, has been left behind. A powerful training technology exists now, but upper management doesn't know about it. What most executives believe about training is based largely on what they experienced in their schooling. Management sets new business goals that require employees to perform in new ways. But the tools upper management knows about simply don't have the power to produce the necessary changes in employee performance. That's why you need to educate managers and executives about CRI.

The payoff? You will bring tools for enhancing employee performance to upper management that are more powerful than they imagined possible. These tools will allow them to implement business strategies with speed and certainty. As training professionals, we must move towards business solutions that take advantage of the potential power of human performance and away from outdated methodologies. *The Path to Smart Training Decisions* ensures that the training programs you provide to your organization produce the changes in performance your organization needs.

Appendix A

Instructional Paradigms:
Academic vs. Business

All too often, people believe that there is only one possible paradigm for instructional programs: the academic paradigm which they experienced in their schooling. Many people are not even aware that there is such a thing as a business instructional paradigm. The chart on the next page breaks down the differences between the two paradigms. In this discussion, you want to lead people to see that there is another legitimate way to design and deliver instruction that meets a totally different set of needs and requirements.

Instructional Paradigms

ACADEMIC   VS.   BUSINESS

PURPOSE

Disseminate information from an authority.	Teach learner to perform a job or part of a job to standard.

ROLE PHILOSOPHY

The instructor provides clear presentations, and the student learns as much as possible.	To provide employees with relevant practice.

PROCESSES

Apply rhetoric and multimedia technology to communicate information.	1. Identify skills that must be learned to perform a job. 2. Design practice conditions for each skill.

EVALUATION

1. One-shot testing. 2. Compare students to each other. 3. Student satisfaction.	1. Try, try again. 2. Ready to move to the next skill. 3. Did they learn the job skills?

UNDERLYING THEORY

The mind is an information repository—like a library or a computer.	The brain is a complex switching system that generates perceptions and performances.

VALUES

1. Differentiates among students. 2. Identifies talented and fast learners. 3. Promises nothing.	All employees succeed in the program and on the job.

HOW WE THINK OF IT

Students gather in a classroom to hear an expert describe and explain his or her knowledge and wisdom.	An instructional process designed, developed, and operated by performance technologists to produce competent job performers.

The academic and business paradigms were developed to serve different needs in different institutions.

- ■ **The academic paradigm** evolved to provide the general population with an opportunity to learn basic academic and socialization skills and culturally valued knowledge *over a period of many years*. It is intended to provide all with an equal opportunity but not with an equal outcome. The educational process extends throughout childhood and early adulthood. How far a particular person proceeds in the educational process largely depends upon how well that person did in earlier phases of the process.

- ■ **The business paradigm** evolved to provide a few selected people with the skills they need to perform competently in particular jobs. The intent of business training is to provide all employees in a particular program with an equal outcome: job competence. Employees are usually away from their jobs while going through an instructional program. This is an expensive arrangement—the employee is being paid but is not producing. Consequently, business instruction not only has to be highly effective, it also has to be highly efficient.

Many of the valued characteristics of the academic paradigm are *counterproductive* in a business environment. Let's see how.

Purpose

The academic paradigm *grew from much earlier times when there were few books, few libraries, and few people who could read. Consequently, the lecture was the only medium for disseminating knowledge to others.*

Later, when it became politically and economically important for the general population to possess academic skills and some established knowledge, the lecture continued as the principal medium for disseminating the desired knowledge. The lecture (by itself or in combination with other media) continues today as the principal activity in academic education at virtually all levels, even though most people have adequate reading skills and other media are readily available. Its use is often rationalized as a motivator of students even though it clearly is not a motivator (Milton 1972).

The principal purpose of the academic paradigm was and continues to be the dissemination of knowledge or information. Specific skills and application problems have been added to the topics in many subject matter areas, and students are required to practice these skills and perform the applications. However, these programs are still organized around the topics that make up the subject matter. Furthermore, they only address a small number of the skills and applications required for competent performance in future situations. They are at best performance-enhanced subject matter (or academic) programs.

The business paradigm *also grew from much earlier times, but it was concerned with learning crafts—that is, learning to* **do** *something that contributed to the productivity of a business enterprise. It has always had a "Watch me do it ... now you do it" flavor to it.*

The focus of the business paradigm is much more on action: the performance of skills, not the understanding of concepts. The business paradigm has been extended in recent decades to include "thinking." Thinking is itself an activity or performance, and consists of talking to yourself and creating internal images. Consequently, thinking skills can be learned in this approach just as readily as physical and perceptual skills.

Role Philosophy

In the academic paradigm, *the dissemination of information takes the form of providing students with clear presentations of that information through lectures and textbooks. Today, the instructor's lectures are usually supplemented with other forms of information presentation.*

The students' role in the academic paradigm is to learn as much of the presented information as possible. How much information the students learn is often measured by tests in which the students discriminate true statements from false ones, complete statements taken from the presentations, or answer essay or discussion questions. However, in many academic programs used in business, no attempt is made to measure how much information the students learn. And that is just as well, since there is typically a low relationship between performance on these kinds of tests and later job performance.

In the business paradigm, *the employees' practice can take many different forms depending upon the kinds of performances that need to be practiced. The employees might do role plays in which they coach a peer,* *operate machinery, prepare business plans and reports, make sales presentations, design products, and so on. Whatever they need to learn to do for the job is what they will practice in training.*

The employees will actually be performing bits and pieces of the job during training. Consequently, each practice situation needs to provide the employee with all the information, materials, and equipment he or she needs to perform that particular piece of the job. Information may include information about the job context in which the skill is performed, about the required specifications for whatever he or she is producing, about safety concerns and practices, and so on.

Processes

The academic paradigm *primarily depends upon processes intended to clearly relate the instructor's material to the students.*

Instructors are often evaluated on the clarity of their presentations and their responses to student questions, even though other media are also used to present information to the students. In fact, the academic paradigm goes through regular media gyrations as new presentation technology is developed. For example, the favored media has moved from chalkboard graphics and film strips to overheads and training films and on to multimedia presentations using laptop computers and LCD projectors just in the last fifty years. Students don't necessarily learn any more today because of these advances than they did when they were taught without them. Yet they command a lion's share of the training budget in many companies that still use the academic paradigm.

The business paradigm: *There are two major processes in the business paradigm.*

1. Techniques to identify the skills needed to learn to do the job. These techniques identify and describe the tasks performed on the job, the skills needed to perform those tasks, and the skills already possessed by the employees to be trained.

2. Techniques for designing practice conditions for each skill that needs to be learned by the employees and for organizing the skills and their practice conditions into coherent training programs.

Evaluation

The academic paradigm: *Most of us remember all too well how the academic paradigm evaluates students.*

- It uses paper and pencil knowledge tests that are easy for the instructor to score.

- Everyone takes the same test at the same time—ready or not.

- Grades are assigned by comparing students to each other on the basis of where each score falls in the class' distribution of scores.

- There is no second chance. Each test is given just once at the appointed time.

Remember the knots in your belly just before and during a test and the sinking feelings of self-doubt following the test? We all do. And to top it off, those tests that caused us so much agony are poor predictors of future performance. So why do schools use these kinds of tests? Because they are easy to administer and score and because they are fair—that is, they mistreat everyone in the same way. They are just not relevant to our future lives.

Since academic programs do not seek to achieve some outcome relevant to future performance, there is no criterion for evaluating them other than student or customer satisfaction. Did the students like the program? Does the paying customer feel he got his money's worth? These are often important questions, but they don't go to the heart of the business issue: Does the training produce competent job performers?

The business paradigm: *The way in which employees are evaluated in the business paradigm is totally different in purpose, process, and procedure.*

The ideal is to evaluate each employee on each skill whenever the employee feels he or she is ready. The purpose of the evaluation is to determine whether the employee is ready to stop practicing the given skill and move on to the next. The employee is ready to move on when he or she meets the job standard for the given skill. What the employee does in practice and what he or she does on the test are identical. A test is simply an observed practice trial. The instructor observes the employee's practice and at some point says: "That meets the job standard. Now you can move on to the next skill."

Business programs do seek to achieve real performance outcomes. The program is evaluated simply by counting the number of employees that demonstrated job competence on all the needed skills. This basic program evaluation is built into all training programs adhering to the business paradigm.

Underlying Theory

The academic paradigm: *The underlying theory of the academic paradigm is somewhat like the line in the old country song: "Shove up your mug and I'll fill up your jug with that good ol' mountain dew."*

Put a funnel in the hole in the top of each student's head and pour in as much elixir of knowledge as each can hold, read the gauge in the student's eyes that tells you how much was poured in, and assign a grade. Different students come with different size vessels and with different motivations to learn.

Today we might use a computer analogy. Students have different size hard drives—from three gigs to thirty-four gigs. We can load more knowledge files into those with the larger hard drives. The computer provides a more modern metaphor but it ignores the real neurology involved in learning just as much as the primitive vessel metaphor does.

The business paradigm: *The early underlying theory for the business paradigm was something like "We learn by doing" or "Practice makes perfect."*

The recent findings of neuroscience support the tenets of the business paradigm: the brain is a performance-generating organ, not an information-processing and storage device. It learns new ways of perceiving and responding to the world around it by going through those new ways. The challenge for training designers is to find the most focused and efficient manner possible. The processes used to develop business programs focus practice on just those skills that are necessary for competency and deliver practice as efficiently as possible.

Values

The academic paradigm *values differentiating students: a few get A's, a few more get B's, a few get C's, and so on.*

If a lot of students get A's, then we have a bad case of "grade inflation," resulting in "watering down the standards." Test performances that yield a "B" in one class might yield an "A" in another, because students are compared to each other rather than to a fixed standard. Grades don't mean much with regard to future performance in the world of work, although they may be fair predictors of future academic performance. Many students (as was the case with Einstein and Edison) may perform poorly in school, but nevertheless can still make solid contributions to society later on.

The academic paradigm is largely designed to be self-serving, using grades to select students who will do well in academic activities at even higher levels of education. It is not nearly as concerned with preparing students to succeed in later life, which may require added talents or even different talents. The academic paradigm makes no promises about the graduates' ability to perform in the world. It testifies only to the graduates' academic talents.

The business paradigm *values having all employees succeed in the training program, because this success will later correlate to even further success on the job.*

During training, employees practice performing job skills and appropriate combinations of those skills. If there is no long delay between their graduation from training and their opportunity to apply the skills they have learned, they will perform competently on the job. There is no learning curve on the job, and there is no problem transferring knowledge from the classroom to the job because they are actually performing the job successfully during training. Consequently, performance is guaranteed.

How We Think of It

The academic paradigm: *The idealized image we usually have of the academic paradigm is that of eager students gathering in a classroom to hear an expert describe and explain his knowledge and wisdom.*

The master challenges the students' intellect and brings out the brightest and most creative talents in each student. It's the legendary Mark Hopkins sitting on one end of a log and the student on the other end. It's Socrates pulling wisdom out of a student by means of Socratic dialectic. It's the master exercising his right of academic freedom to challenge the students to see important issues in a new light.

The idealized image of the academic paradigm is mostly fantasy. Few of us have ever experienced it. And there certainly aren't many people who can teach in this mode and still manage to meet all the teaching needs in education— much less in business. Even if there were enough teachers with this kind of skill, the approach simply doesn't work well. It can be a heady experience for the student, but it won't necessarily make him a competent performer after he graduates.

The business paradigm: *The idealized image of the business paradigm is that of a learning process designed, developed, and operated by performance technologists to guide employees in learning the skills they need to become competent at performing a job.*

It can take many different forms—from an employee practicing alone following a performance guide to a small group of employees being led by an instructor through pre-designed exercises. They learn and practice on the job or they return to their jobs at the completion of training, where they apply the skills they have just learned in situations similar to those in which they have been practicing.

Appendix B

How People Really Learn
(With Implications for Training)

In 1924, John Watson, the father of behaviorism, relegated the brain to a "black box," declaring that we had no reliable way of learning how it worked. In the early sixties, a new group of scientists called "cognitivists" came along and maintained that they *could* study the mind. However, they never opened John Watson's "black box." Instead, they built elegant theories based on an erroneous assumption: that the mind works like a computer. As we shall see, it is a misleading assumption. How the brain actually works means a great deal for training.

The chart on the following page, "How People Really Learn," prompts you to refute the most common myth in our culture about how our brains work: the computer analogy. It leads to discussions on how the brain thinks, remembers, and learns. It prompts you to explain the major implication for training design of how brains work and how criterion-referenced instruction responds to this implication in the design of employee practice. Finally, it prompts you to explain how the delivery of brain-oriented training differs from the delivery of academic instruction. The following talking points offer some additional support for the chart.

How People Really Learn

With Implications for Training

THE OLD VIEW VS.	THE NEW VIEW
THE BRAIN	
The brain is like a computer. It stores and retrieves information to and from various kinds of memories.	The brain builds neural circuits that perceive sensory inputs and generate movements in response to those inputs.
THINKING	
Thinking is computation performed on an underlying and unknown mental code. The results are then decoded into language and imagery.	Thinking is an inner dialogue that consists of language and imagery. It is learned like any other skill—through practice with feedback.
REMEMBERING	
Remembering consists of retrieving encoded information from memory. The information is then decoded into language and imagery.	Remembering consists of activating some of the neural circuits used in a previous experience to produce a similar response (memory). It is context-sensitive.
LEARNING	
Learning consists of storing and retrieving information to and from various memories.	Learning consists of assembling existing neural circuits into new ones to generate new perceptions and movements. "Neurons that fire together wire together."
INSTRUCTIONAL DEVELOPMENT	
Instructional development consists of selecting subject matter, preparing presentations using various media, and developing supplementary practice exercises.	Instructional development consists of identifying job performances, analyzing them into activities that need to be learned, and developing practice conditions for each activity.
INSTRUCTIONAL DELIVERY	
Instructional delivery consists of providing information in presentations (lectures, textbooks, and media) to the students and providing supplementary practice exercises.	Instructional delivery consists of leading students through performing the activities they need to learn (including the inner dialogues of thinking) until they can perform the activities without prompting.

The Brain

Our culture depicts our brains as organs that store memories of the significant events that occur to us. In reality, our brains guide us through life events using "means" they have developed in past events. The brain builds pathways by stringing neurons together to channel signals from sensory inputs to motor outputs. Neural structures are more way stations than storage facilities—transforming and redirecting a flow of signals to activate the appropriate response organs. When viewed this way, the brain is magnificently intricate but not nearly so clever.

It is the "means" by which we deal with life events—not descriptions of the life events themselves. These "means" are ways of perceiving incoming sensory signals and ways of responding to them. When we think or remember, we use many of the same neural pathways that we use when we perceive or respond to events in the world around us. Basically, we engage in interplay of words and images organized by pathways in other parts of the brain.

Thinking

Thinking is largely what we experience it to be: activating imagery, talking to ourselves about the imagery, and activating more imagery with the words we use in talking to ourselves. This cycle goes on endlessly. Effective thinking is learned largely through rehearsal, but not verbatim rehearsal. It has to use the imagery and language circuits that already exist in the thinker. Such rehearsal, however, can be guided with images and words from another person, a printed performance guide, or some other source. Furthermore, it needs to be rehearsed in the same performance context in which it will later be applied.

Remembering

If there is no memory where we store records of all the events of our past, then how do we remember these things? Basically, we talk to ourselves and others about the event during and after its occurrence. The words we speak conjure up inner images and the images, in turn, lead to more words. As we repeat these verbal and imagery performances over time, they become our record of the event. Many of our memories are, in fact, rehearsed performances. Bits and pieces of these records are used in many other performances and often become changed in the process. When next we remember, we might use those same bits and pieces that have now become changed in small ways. That's part of how we misremember. Ongoing activity in the brain often modifies how we reconstruct a given memory or chain of thoughts at any particular moment.

The same cues for recalling a given memory on two different occasions may lead to different memories on different occasions because of differences in ongoing mental activities.

Learning

What happens in our brain when we learn? Learning consists of modifying old pathways or building new ones. How does the brain build new pathways? Hebb's Law establishes how new pathways are built or modified. In popular form, it says: "Neurons that fire together wire together." Every new experience produces changes in the pathways in our brains. These changes provide us with pathways for dealing with similar experiences in our future.

The pathways that change when we learn include those that generate our body movements. That's easily understood as long as we are talking about dancing or athletics. But how about operating a computer? How do I know what commands to find in a particular menu of an application? If you ask me, can I tell you? Probably not. But if I sit down at the computer with the application running, I can tell you quickly. Moving the cursor under my control makes all the difference in the world. Moving the cursor is part of how I "know" the application. Body movements provide sensory signals to our brains that are as important to learning as signals from the world around us. We are not consciously aware of the sensory signals coming from our muscles and joints, but clearly they are there or we could not coordinate our movements. They can also be critical for driving other parts of the bigger pathway.

Remember when you counted on your fingers? Ticking off the fingers with the thumb and then ticking off the thumb with a hand gesture were movements that generated signals in muscles and joints that in turn triggered your saying the next number to yourself. Was this counting a cognitive act or a motor act? It doesn't make any difference what you call it as long as you keep in mind what was happening. Body movements and the resulting sensory inputs are critical to much of what we know.

Instructional Development

The whole point of training should be to connect new pathways in employees' brains that generate the performances they need for job competence. Criterion-referenced instruction leads employees through doing the things they need to learn to do. This is how we fire all the right neurons together to wire them together. Training provides employees with the conditions they need to practice doing bits and pieces of the job they need to learn to do. The job, bit by bit, is recreated in the practice situations that make up the training program.

How should the training lead employees through doing those things they need to learn to do?

- We must specify the job performances we want employees to learn to do.

- We must break those job performances down successively into their component activities (including mental activities) until we reach the level of skill already possessed by the employees.

- We must develop situations that lead employees through *doing* those things we want them to learn to do.

- We must lead employees through practicing the new activities, beginning with the lowest level and successively assembling higher-level activities from lower-level components.

- We must provide employees with sufficient practice at each level to establish permanently connected neural circuits.

Criterion-referenced instruction is a highly efficient form of learning by doing.

Instructional Delivery

Criterion-referenced instruction is based on the new view of the brain as a performance-generating organ. It results in graduates who are fully competent to do the job at graduation.

Traditional instruction is based on the old view of the brain as an information processing and storage device. It results in graduates who are far from competent at the time of graduation. They are left with a great deal to learn on the job, which is not an efficient way to learn. Most graduates eventually achieve competence, but a few never do. The learning curve on the job extends from months to years. The lack of fully competent performance during the learning curve is costly to the company not only in lost productivity but also in poor quality output and loss of customer confidence.

Appendix C

Criterion-Referenced Instruction for Today's Business Needs

A recent study by the American Society for Training and Development of over 2575 firms gives managers and executives incentive to make training a priority. The ASTD study provides definitive evidence that training investments can yield favorable financial returns for firms and their investors.

When ranked according to how much they spent on training, firms in the top half [of the study group] had a total shareholder return that was 86 percent higher than firms in the bottom half, and 45 percent higher than the market average..... Firms in the top quarter of the study, as measured by average per-employee expenditures on training, enjoyed **higher profit margins** (by 24 percent), **higher income per employee** (by 218 percent), and **higher price-to-book ratios** (by 26 percent) on average than firms in the bottom quarter (ASTD 2000).

As the ASTD study shows, training can have a large financial impact on an organization. But to be effective, the training has to work. It has to guarantee that learners will master job-critical skills and gain the self-confidence to perform to management expectations. Criterion-referenced instruction (CRI) is the only training methodology that can meet this critical business need. CRI is a way of managing and organizing instruction so that each participant performs to pre-specified criteria before completing training. Each training objective is derived from a specific job performance need. Participants are given the opportunity to practice the skills they are learning and demonstrate competence in each objective.

With training developed using CRI, you can guarantee that each trainee will have the skills to perform at the level of proficiency required on Day 1 after training. CRI can also result in **lower training costs** and **reduced training time**, and it provides great flexibility in choosing methods of delivery. Some recent results of CRI include:

- Due to the implementation of a CRI-based training program at a paper mill, "One paper machine realized **annual savings of $169,000** based on the development of new refiner start-up procedures. This occurred after a needs analysis identified operator skill deficiencies—particularly in the area of abnormal operating conditions. After the mill designed, developed, and implemented skill-specific CRI modules, refiner start-up problems were eliminated..... CRI typically **reduce[d] the time needed for training by 38% to 70%**, eliminating the need for 12-hour shifts to accommodate training" (PIMA's Papermaker December 1998).

- Caterpillar Americas, the Latin American commercial subsidiary of Caterpillar Inc., developed a CRI-based program to improve individual sales force performance. In one year, **"won back" customers increased by 341%**, while **new customers increased by 225%**. The CRI-based program resulted in a two year total sales value of **$95 million** (1997 Annual Quality Improvement Report, Caterpillar Inc.).

- At Honda Canada, implementation of the CRI methodology reduced skills training time required from **7 months to 2 months**. While the number of new models being launched tripled, the efficiency of CRI-based training resulted in all dealer technicians being successfully trained on the new models without the need for additional training staff (CRI Application Conference 2000).

The differences between criterion-referenced instruction and other instructional development methodologies lie with CRI's use of analysis. With CRI, analysis is used throughout the design and development process to identify:

- Desired performance,

- All skills that will be required to achieve desired performance,

- The most effective and efficient methods for achieving desired performance, and

- Potential problems that may arise.

Another fundamental of CRI that distinguishes it from traditional methodologies is its flexibility. CRI training is developed in modules (or units of instruction) that can be delivered in a variety of ways, including a self-paced format. Therefore, the delivery method can be dictated by the needs of the target population, the realities of the environment, and/or the specifications of the skills being taught, rather than by the nature of the course design.

Some additional principles of CRI that make it unique include:

- **Relevant practice**—To successfully apply skills learned in training back on the job, trainees must practice them and gain confidence in their ability to perform them in situations that closely resemble the environment in which the skills will be applied. CRI-developed training provides this practice, enabling trainees to apply their skills immediately upon return to their jobs.

- **Demonstration of competence**—Unlike more conventional forms of instruction, CRI focuses on application of knowledge rather than retention of it. Without the ability to transfer knowledge into the skills necessary for achieving desired performance, knowledge has little value. With training developed using CRI, each trainee must demonstrate his or her ability to not only perform each skill training is designed to teach but to perform it at the level of proficiency management requires.

- **Exclusion of irrelevant content**—CRI-developed training includes only knowledge that is essential for learners to achieve desired performance—no more, no less. This efficiency can reduce training times and result in significant dollar savings.

Over the years, use of the CRI methodology has grown along with its reputation for giving organizations the power to achieve the performance results they need. From the hospitality, service, healthcare, and financial industries to the pharmaceutical, manufacturing, and automotive industries, organizations are using CRI to ensure their workforces have all the skills to perform at the levels of proficiency required.

Appendix D

The Path to Smart Training Decisions Flowchart & Worksheet

The Path to Smart Training Decisions

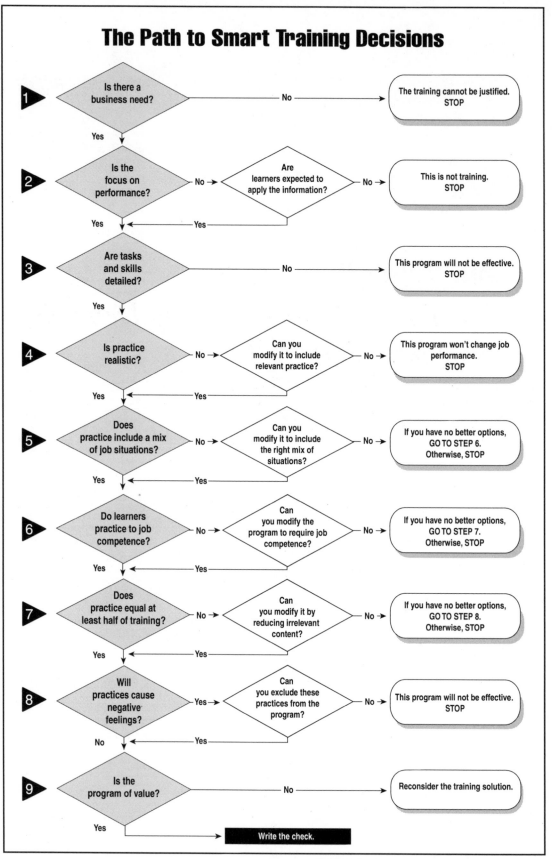

The Path to Smart Training Decisions

STEP 1. IS THERE A BUSINESS NEED?

Is there a substantial need for new training? Is the training program part of one of the following situations?

- Preparing new employees
- Enhancing the performance of current employees with needed skills they don't currently possess
- Implementing business strategies (such as new processes or systems, culture change, restructuring, downsizing) which will require employees to acquire new skills

YES → Complete the **Training Program Identification,** then **GO TO STEP 2**

NO → This training cannot be justified. **STOP**

TRAINING PROGRAM IDENTIFICATION

Program title: _____

Source: _____

Describe the business need this program addresses:

_____
_____
_____
_____
_____
_____
_____

Examples: Build a new corporate culture, increase production, implement TQM, establish work teams.

What position(s) will be trained? _____

_____
_____

Number of employees to be trained: _____

_____
_____

Gender: _____% Male _____% Female

Location(s) of employees: _____

_____

_____

General level of education:
❏ High school   ❏ Undergraduate   ❏ Graduate or higher

Primary language(s): _____

_____

General turnover rate: _____%

Other defining characteristics: _____

_____

_____

_____

_____

_____

_____

_____

_____

_____

STEP 2. IS THE FOCUS ON PERFORMANCE?

Does the program focus on things you want trainees to *do* that they aren't able to do now?

YES→ Briefly identify the desired performances.

Reminder: Performances are described with action verbs and their outcomes.

Examples: Prepare a budget, coach a direct report, facilitate a meeting, troubleshoot and repair a machine, assemble components at a production station, probe a client's needs.

_____

_____

_____

_____

When complete, **GO TO STEP 3**

NO → Is there an expectation that the presented information will be applied on the job? Are some attributes expected to change as a result of the training program?

> **YES** → Arrange to have a performance technologist make the hidden performances visible. Identify technologist(s).
>
> _____
> _____

GO TO STEP 3

> **NO** → This training cannot be justified. If the focus is on presenting information, this is an information session, not a training program. Do not try to turn it into training. **STOP**

STEP 3. ARE TASKS AND SKILLS DETAILED?

Have the specific job tasks and skills needed by the target employees been named and described in detail? If not, will they be?

YES → GO TO STEP 4

NO → Put your checkbook away. This program will not be effective. **STOP**

STEP 4. IS PRACTICE REALISTIC?

Will employees practice the job skills they need to learn in realistic job contexts?

YES → GO TO STEP 5

NO → Can you get the program modified to provide relevant practice?

> **YES** → How will the practice be modified?
>
> _____
> _____
> _____
> _____

> When complete, **GO TO STEP 5**

Can you get the program modified to provide relevant practice?

NO → Put your checkbook away. This training cannot be justified. This program may look glitzy and the employees may like it, but it won't change their job performance. **STOP**

STEP 5. DOES PRACTICE INCLUDE A MIX OF JOB SITUATIONS?

Is practice provided in a representative mix of job situations?

YES → **GO TO STEP 6**

NO → Can you get the program modified by adding representative practice situations drawn from a reasonable inventory of job situations?

> **YES** → Note what practice needs to be added.
>
> _____
> _____
> _____
> _____
> _____
> _____
> _____
> _____
> _____

When complete, **GO TO STEP 6**

> **NO** → This program may work, but there will be a learning curve on the job. If you have no better options, **GO TO STEP 6**. Otherwise, **STOP**

STEP 6. DO LEARNERS PRACTICE TO JOB COMPETENCE?

Will each employee's job competence in each skill be verified during the program?

YES → **GO TO STEP 7**

NO → Can you get the program modified to require the demonstration of job competence by each employee on every skill?

    YES → How will the program be modified?

    _____
    _____
    _____
    _____
    _____
    _____

    When complete, **GO TO STEP 7**

    NO → This program may work, but not well. It does not assure that employees will have a high sense of self-efficacy when they go back to their jobs, and you won't be able to prove to management (or yourself) that it works until you add relevant measurements. If you have no better options, **GO TO STEP 7.** Otherwise, **STOP**

STEP 7. DOES PRACTICE EQUAL AT LEAST HALF OF TRAINING?

Is the program efficient? Will each employee spend at least half of his or her time practicing needed skills?

YES → **GO TO STEP 8**

NO → Can you get the program modified by reducing irrelevant content or by adding practice time if all content is relevant?

    YES → List what content could be eliminated.

    _____
    _____
    _____
    _____
    _____
    _____
    _____

    When complete, **GO TO STEP 8**

Can you get·the program modified by reducing irrelevant content or by adding practice time if all content is relevant?

NO → This program will work, but it will require more time than necessary and confuse some employees. If you have no better options, **GO TO STEP 8**. Otherwise, **STOP**

STEP 8. WILL PRACTICES CAUSE NEGATIVE FEELINGS?

Are the instructional practices likely to produce anxiety, embarrassment, or frustration?

YES→ Can you exclude these practices from the program?

YES → Note how they will be excluded and/or replaced with more suitable practice.

_____
_____
_____
_____
_____
_____

When complete, **GO TO STEP 9**

NO → This program will take longer than necessary, and it will create disgruntled employees. **STOP**

NO → **GO TO STEP 9**

STEP 9. IS THE PROGRAM OF VALUE?

Complete the following worksheet to determine if the benefits of the program outweigh the costs.

Optimal Program Benefit

1. What are the expected financial gains from the success of the business strategy that the program addresses (profits per year)?

   1 _____

2. Conservatively estimate what percentage of the expected gains from the business strategy (see line 1) can be credited to the success of just this training program. Use the space below for any calculations.

   2 _____ %

3. Multiply line 1 and line 2. This is the annual benefit which can be attributed to the strategy.

   3 _____

4. What is the expected benefit life of the program (in years)?

   4 _____

5. Multiply line 3 and line 4. This is the optimal benefit attributable to the training over the life of the program.

   5 _____

Expected Training Effectiveness

6a. What proportion of the program's skills will graduates be able to perform to standard at graduation?

   6a _____ %

6b. What proportion of the program's skills will graduates be able to perform to standard six months after graduation?

   6b _____ %

6c. Average these two proportions. This is the expected
effectiveness of the training program.

6c _____%

Training Benefit

7. Multiply line 5 and line 6c. This is the expected
net benefit of the training program.

7 _____

Actual Training Program Cost

8. How much will the program cost to acquire and
to maintain over the life of the program? Use the
space below to make these calculations. Consider
all upfront costs **and** all ongoing maintenance and
delivery costs.

8 _____

Value of the Training Program

9. Value = Benefits − Costs. Subtract line 8 (cost)
from line 7 (net training benefits). This number
represents the value of the training program. If it is
zero or negative, the training cannot be justified,
and you need to reconsider the solution.

9 _____

10. Calculate the benefit/cost ratio by dividing line 7 by
line 8.

10 _____

It's up to you to determine whether the ratio in line
10 indicates that the program is worthwhile.
However, it's probably safe to assume that you're
not in the ballpark if the ratio is only marginally
greater than 1:1. In that case, you need to evaluate
whether this is the best return for your investment.
Is there a way to get the most benefit for
proportionally less cost? Be prepared to answer
some questions. You need to be certain that this is
the best return for your dollar.

References

Bandura, Albert. 1986. *Social Foundations of Thought and Action.* Englewood Cliffs, NJ: Prentice-Hall.

Damasio, Antonio R. 1994. *Descartes' Error: Emotion, Reason, and the Human Brain.* New York: Grossett/Putnam, G.P. Putnam's Sons.

Edelman, Gerald M. 1992. Mind without biology: A critical postscript. In *Bright Air, Brilliant Fire: On the Matter of the Mind.* New York: BasicBooks.

Loftus, Elizabeth F. 1997. Creating false memories. *Scientific American* (September).

Mager, Robert F. 1997a. *Goal Analysis: How to clarify your goals so you can actually achieve them.* 3d ed. Atlanta: The Center for Effective Performance, Inc.

_____. 1997b. *Making Instruction Work: A step-by-step guide to designing and developing instruction that works.* 2d ed. Atlanta: The Center for Effective Performance, Inc.

Mager, Robert F. and Peter Pipe. 1994. *Criterion-Referenced Instruction: Practical Skills for Designing Instruction That Works.* 4th ed. Atlanta: The Center for Effective Performance, Inc.

Milton, Ohmer. 1972. *Alternatives to the Traditional.* San Francisco: Jossey-Bass Publishers, Inc.

Phillips, Jack J. 1997. *Return on Investment in Training and Performance Improvement Programs.* Oxford: Butterworth-Heinemann.

Index

CEP WORKSHOPS

CEP offers *the* industry-standard Mager Workshops for training and performance improvement professionals. Our workshops don't just tell you about CRI-based instruction; we teach you how to *apply* the methodology to training projects.

Criterion-Referenced Instruction by Robert F. Mager and Peter Pipe
The CRI Methodology Part 1: Analysis, Design and Evaluation

The Criterion-Referenced Instruction workshop will give you immediately applicable, practical skills in analysis, design and evaluation necessary to succeed in a state-of-the-art training and performance improvement department. You'll learn how to:

- Conduct in-depth analysis (including goal, performance and task analyses)
- Edit and derive clear and measurable objectives
- Draft effective procedural guides, skill checks, course scenarios and course maps
- Plan course evaluations
- Quickly evaluate existing materials and plan course improvements

Instructional Module Development by Robert F. Mager
The CRI Methodology Part 2: Development

In the follow-up workshop to CRI, you build on your CRI skills to:

- Draft, try out and revise at least two modules of instruction for a course you are developing
- Test modules with other participants
- Experience firsthand the tryout process from the student' point of view
- Learn by seeing instruction in a variety of formats and subject areas

The Training Manager Workshop by Robert F. Mager

Learn how to support the achievement of your organization's strategic goals by providing employees with the skills and motivation to perform their jobs to management's expectations. During the workshop, you will work on the following modules:

- Evaluate instructors' performance
- Evaluate proposals for services
- Plan course evaluations
- Review training development progress
- Assess media choices
- Review training modules
- Solve performance problems
- Identify job tasks
- Create effective objectives
- Identify prerequisite skills

For more information and a schedule of public workshops, visit www.cepworldwide.com or call us at 1-800-558-4CEP

More Great Books from CEP PRESS

CEP Press is a full-service publisher of performance improvement, training, and management books and tools. All of our publications boast the same high quality and value, and the same practical resources and relevant information that you have come to expect from our world-renowned publications. **Order your copies today and get resources you'll use for a lifetime.**

	Quantity	Price	Total
How to Make Smart Decisions About Training: Save Money, Time & Frustration by Paul G. Whitmore **($22.95 US, $35.95 CAN)**			
The Bottomline on ROI: Basics, Benefits & Barriers to Measuring Training & Performance Improvement by Patricia Pulliam Phillips, Series Editor Jack J. Phillips Available in February 2002 **($16.95 US, $24.95 CAN)**			
Making an Impact: Building a Top-Performing Organization from the Bottom Up by Timm J. Esque **($16.95 US, $24.95 CAN)**			
What Every Manager Should Know About Training by Robert F. Mager & Peter Pipe **($22.95 US, $35.95 CAN)**			
The New Mager 6-Pack The reference library for educators, trainers, or anyone serious about improving performance by Robert F. Mager **($115 US, $179.95 CAN)**			
Goal Analysis: How to clarify your goals so you can actually achieve them by Robert F. Mager **($22.95 US, $35.95 CAN)**			
Subtotal			
Shipping & Handling			
GA residents add 7% sales tax to the subtotal plus S&H. Canada and TX residents add applicable sales tax to the subtotal plus S&H.			
TOTAL ORDER			

U.S. Shipping & Handling: Please add $6 for the first book plus $1.50 for each additional book. Please allow four weeks for delivery by ground delivery.

Name _____

Phone _____ **Fax** _____

Organization _____

Address _____

City _____ **State** _____ **ZIP** _____

❑ My check for $_____ is enclosed.

Charge my ❑ Visa ❑ Mastercard ❑ AmEx   Exp. Date _____

Card Number _____

Name on Card _____

Please send this form and your check or credit card number to:
CEP, P.O. Box 102462, Atlanta, GA 30368-2462

Call 1-800-558-4CEP for volume discount information and for shipping charges on international orders. For credit card orders, fax this order for faster delivery to (770) 458-9109 or use our Web site: www.ceppress.com